T0358196

Cambridge Elements ≡

Elements in Politics and Society in Southeast Asia
edited by
Edward Aspinall
Australian National University
Meredith L. Weiss
University at Albany, SUNY

THE PHILIPPINES

From "People Power" to Democratic Backsliding

Mark R. Thompson
City University of Hong Kong

CAMBRIDGE
UNIVERSITY PRESS

Shaftesbury Road, Cambridge CB2 8EA, United Kingdom

One Liberty Plaza, 20th Floor, New York, NY 10006, USA

477 Williamstown Road, Port Melbourne, VIC 3207, Australia

314–321, 3rd Floor, Plot 3, Splendor Forum, Jasola District Centre,
New Delhi – 110025, India

103 Penang Road, #05–06/07, Visioncrest Commercial, Singapore 238467

Cambridge University Press is part of Cambridge University Press & Assessment,
a department of the University of Cambridge.

We share the University's mission to contribute to society through the pursuit of
education, learning and research at the highest international levels of excellence.

www.cambridge.org
Information on this title: www.cambridge.org/9781009398480

DOI: 10.1017/9781009398466

First published 2023

A catalogue record for this publication is available from the British Library.

ISBN 978-1-009-39848-0 Paperback
ISSN 2515-2998 (online)
ISSN 2515-298X (print)

The Philippines

From "People Power" to Democratic Backsliding

Elements in Politics and Society in Southeast Asia

DOI: 10.1017/9781009398466
First published online: May 2023

Mark R. Thompson
City University of Hong Kong

Author for correspondence: Mark R. Thompson, mark.thompson@cityu.edu.hk

Abstract: This Element explores how in the Philippines a "whiggish" narrative of democracy and good governance triumphing over dictatorship and kleptocracy after the "people power" uprising against Ferdinand E. Marcos in 1986 was upended by strongman Rodrigo R. Duterte three decades later. Portraying his father's authoritarian rule as a "golden age," Ferdinand R. Marcos, Jr. succeeded Duterte by easily winning the 2022 presidential election, suggesting democratic backsliding will persist. A structuralist account of the inherent instability of the country's oligarchical democracy offers a plausible explanation of repeated crises but underplays agency. Strategic groups have pushed back against executive aggrandizement. Offering a "structuration" perspective, presidential power and elite pushback are examined as is the reliance on political violence and the instrumentalization of mass poverty. These factors have recurrently combined to lead to the fall, restoration, and now steep decline of democracy in the Philippines.

Keywords: Philippines, democratic backsliding, patronage, political violence, development

ISBNs: 9781009398480 (PB), 9781009398466 (OC)
ISSNs: 2515-2998 (online), 2515-298X (print)

Contents

1 Introduction

The Philippine "people power" uprising in Metro Manila in February 1986 captivated the global media. Said to be the first popular uprising broadcast on live television around the world, it also garnered praise from many world leaders (although less enthusiastically from US President Ronald Reagan, a long-time friend of Philippine dictator Ferdinand E. Marcos and his wife Imelda Romualdez Marcos) (Bonner 1987). People power demonstrated that an authoritarian ruler could be overthrown peacefully by civilian protesters demanding democratic restoration. Among its iconic images were nuns holding flowers and kneeling in front of government soldiers (for a hagiographic account see Mercado 1986; for a critical perspective see Claudio 2013). Even where the Philippine origins of the term have been forgotten, people power became a template for pro-democracy uprisings in Asia – in South Korea in 1987, Myanmar in 1988, China in 1989, Indonesia in 1998 – and beyond, with former dissident and Czech president Václav Havel thanking Filipinos for helping inspire the 1989 central European democratic revolutions (Kulkarni and Tasker 1996; Thompson 2004, 18).[1]

But within the Philippines itself, the perception of people power has undergone a remarkable metamorphosis. Corazon "Cory" C. Aquino, the widow of assassinated opposition politician Benigno "Ninoy" S. Aquino, Jr., who became president after the heavily manipulated snap presidential elections of early February 1986 that sparked the uprising, died in 2009. There was a national outpouring of grief at the huge funeral held for *tita* (auntie) Cory who had led the restoration of democracy. The necropolitical impact of her death soon became apparent. "Noynoy" S. Aquino III, a surprise entrant to the 2010 presidential campaign, promised to continue his mother's and father's legacy (one of his most frequently aired campaign commercials featured him speaking reassuringly with pictures of them smiling behind him). Promising to strengthen democracy, promote good governance, and aid the poor, Noynoy Aquino easily won a plurality in a multicandidate field (without a second French-style round) on the wave of sympathy following his mother's death. But this second Aquino presidency was much diminished by a major (but typical) patronage-related scandal and continued high poverty levels. This appeared to invalidate both the conditional claim and predicted result of Noynoy Aquino's campaign slogan: "*Kung walang corrupt, walang mahirap*" ("If there is no corruption, then there will be no poor").

---

[1] In this sense, the Philippines arguably had *the* "modular revolution" (Beissinger 2007) of that period in Asia, establishing a paradigm for "democratic revolutions" (Thompson 2004, chp. 1).

When Noynoy Aquino died in 2021, public reaction was decidedly mixed. Some social posts showed yellow ribbons hung in high-end neighborhoods (the ribbons were inspired by the popular song "Tie a Yellow Ribbon Round the Ole Oak Tree" and referred to the welcome planned by supporters of his father, Ninoy Aquino, before he was assassinated upon his return from exile in August 1983). But several influential social media influencers who were strong backers of his successor, Rodrigo R. Duterte, openly bashed the deceased despite the strong Philippine taboo of not speaking ill of the dead (Ranada 2021a).

Duterte's election in 2016 demonstrated a "whiggish" narrative of democracy triumphing over authoritarianism and good governance supplanting blatant kleptocracy had been upended. Instead of a benighted dictatorial past, the democratic present had become an object of scorn. This trend continued with Ferdinand R. Marcos, Jr.'s landslide victory in the May 2022 presidential election, winning twice as many votes as his nearest rival, Maria Leonor "Leni" Robredo, the outgoing vice president with close links to the Aquinos. She changed her campaign color to pink, implicitly acknowledging the unpopularity of the "yellow" political brand (Tiglao 2022b; Thompson 2022c). Marcos, by contrast, unapologetically ran on the promise to restore the "golden age" his father's authoritarian rule supposedly represented (Talamayan 2021; Curato 2022).

Duterte convinced many Filipinos they had been betrayed by irresponsible "yellow" elites. Similar to how Donald Trump beat Hillary Clinton in the US presidential campaign later that same year, the populist insurgent Duterte effectively portrayed Aquino's preferred successor – close friend, cabinet member, and fellow scion Manuel "Mar" Araneta Roxas, II – as incompetent, soft on crime, and out of touch with ordinary people (Thompson 2018). Roxas found the rhetoric of liberal reformism no longer resonated, instead seeming sanctimonious and hypocritical.

As Duterte had promised, as president he immediately launched a "war on drugs" with thousands of extrajudicial killings by police and police-linked vigilantes. In late 2018, the chair of the Philippine Commission on Human Rights estimated that as many as 27,000 suspected drug users and dealers had been killed in the drug war (Maru 2018). Several months earlier, the Republic of the Philippines Supreme Court (2018, 48) noted that the Duterte administration had reported 20,322 homicides during its drug war from July 1, 2016, to November 27, 2017, leading the court to ask why "so many deaths had happened" in the government's "'Fighting Illegal Drugs'" campaign, which amounted to a staggering average of over forty per day during this period. A 2020 UN report found "widespread and systematic extrajudicial killings" in the anti-drug campaign in which there was "near-impunity for such violations" (United Nations High Commissioner on Human Rights 2020, 6). The number and manner of the killings bordered on the genocidal (Simangan 2018).

In addition, Duterte targeted mayors and local officials accused of having drug links – by June 2021 more than half of the forty-four mayors, vice mayors, and other local officials identified by the Philippine president as being "narco politicians" had been killed (Gutierrez 2021; also Kreuzer 2020). Duterte had opposition senator Leila de Lima jailed on dubious drug charges after she had led an upper house investigation of his drug war. He also attacked the independent media (noted journalist and Nobel Peace Prize winner Maria Ressa has faced numerous court cases with her online newspaper *Rappler* threatened with closure while the country's most popular TV station, ABS-CBN, was forced off the air after its license was not renewed by Duterte's congressional allies).

Yet Duterte claimed democratic legitimacy despite his obvious illiberalism (Thompson 2021). Literally sticking to his guns by fulfilling his drug war campaign promise, he became the most popular president since people power, with his satisfaction rating reaching a record high of over 90 percent (Ranada 2021b). Alongside his high poll ratings, his allies shut out all oppositional senatorial candidates in the 2019 midterm elections for the first time in nearly a century (Hutchcroft 2019). Promising continuity with the Duterte administration, Marcos, Jr., with Duterte's daughter Sara Duterte-Carpio as his vice presidential running mate, swept the 2022 presidential polls (Arguelles 2022).

"*Dilawan*" (yellowed) – as pro-Aquino supporters are disparagingly referred to by Duterte and Marcos backers – are portrayed as out of touch. Their human rights discourse as well as promises of political reform and anti-poverty programs are no longer believable as corruption has persisted, institutions are still weak, and the majority of Filipinos have remained poor. Duterte's obscenity-ridden, vulgar speaking style underlined his political authenticity (Abinales 2015; Szilágyi and Thompson 2016; Curato and Ong 2018; Montiel, Uyheng, and de Leon 2021). He was widely seen as calling out the hypocrisy of traditional "political elites using his coarse language" (Contreras 2020, 67).

Parallels to the Global Wave of Illiberal Populism

Duterte's illiberalism reflected larger global trends (McCoy 2017). Yet unlike Trump and right-wing populists in developed countries who target immigrants, Duterte identified drug users and dealers as "enemies of the people." More than just the "penal populism" common in the West (Pratt 2006), Duterte's violent populism was a particularly virulent form of illiberal rule that took the aggressive intent of the "us versus them" polarity to its deadly extreme (Thompson 2022a). Through his "war on drugs," Duterte won massive popular support, the extent of which other illiberal populists globally – who had a mobilized base but often lacked broad public backing – could only dream (Kenny 2020).

This wave of illiberal populism – characterized by an exclusionary ideology pitting "good people" against a corrupt elite coddling minorities and outcasts (Wodak 2015; Judis 2016) – reached Southeast Asia relatively late. Having won a sweeping victory in parliamentary elections in 2001 on a populist platform, Prime Minister Thaksin Shinawatra launched a brief war on drugs in Thailand in mid-2003, which purportedly targeted criminals but was actually directed at factional political rivals before the Thai politician returned to his pro-poor rhetoric (Prajak 2014, 395–397). In 2014 and 2019, Prabowo Subianto's intolerant Islamist-tinged populism nearly won him the Indonesian presidency (Mietzner 2014; Aspinall and Mietzner 2019). But without doubt it was Duterte's election in 2016 with his promise to throw thousands of bodies of murdered drug criminals in Manila Bay "until the fish grew fat" that brought illiberal populism in Southeast Asia to the world's attention (Teehankee and Thompson 2016; McCoy 2017; Heydarian 2018). Once elected, Duterte unleashed police vigilantes in a nationally directed but locally conducted killing spree in the name of a war on drugs. He later also enabled the military's targeting of legal leftists "red tagged" as communists (Beltran 2020). He eroded democracy in less violent ways as well, undercutting judicial independence, marginalizing independent institutions, and bullying local leaders (Deinla, Taylor, and Rood 2018; Dressel and Bonoan 2019; Gera and Hutchcroft 2021).

While many contemporary illiberal populist leaders have excluded, imprisoned, or even assassinated those othered by their rhetoric, only Duterte instigated state-led mass murder against his country's own civilian population through his war on drugs. While Turkey's Recep Erdoğan intensified attacks against Kurdish rebels and Russia's Vladimir Putin waged the brutal Second Chechen War and has now invaded Ukraine, these are military campaigns, not "peacetime" massacres. Thaksin's drug war has been compared to Duterte's crackdown (Janjira and Arugay 2016; Raffle 2021). But a commission set up after Thaksin had been toppled classified only fifty-four deaths as "extrajudicial killings" during this short period (Ferrara 2015, 228–229), relatively few when set beside the tens of thousands estimated to have been murdered during Duterte's anti-drug campaign during his six-year term in office (United Nations High Commissioner on Human Rights 2020).

A Structuralist Perspective

Sidel (2016) has suggested, following Hedman (2006), that "Duterte's election to the presidency is the latest iteration of a cyclical pattern in Philippine politics." About every fifteen years the "normal pattern" of electoral competition between "virtually indistinguishable representatives of the country's oligarchy" is interrupted by a "critical juncture." This is due to the "aspirations, grievances, conflicts and tensions" that "build up to challenge the narrow constraints and limitations of oligarchical democracy" (Sidel 2016). Analyzing Marcos' declaration of martial law in 1972, Nowak and Snyder (1974) identified the major reason for the breakdown of democracy as capitalist commercialization which undermined the material basis for traditional patron–client relations, raising the cost of campaigning, making it more difficult to integrate poor voters, and leading to the rise of mass mobilization as well as elite counterreaction. In an influential article, Benedict Anderson (1988) traced the origins of landlord-dominated "cacique democracy" to US colonial rule which concentrated land, and economic resources generally, in the hands of a small elite who built local political dynasties through elections held under "colonial democracy" (Paredes 1989). As Anderson (1988) argued, it was only a matter of time before a "Supreme Cacique" in the person of Marcos arose, putting an end to the electoral game by declaring martial law in 1972. The fall of the Marcos dictatorship, like earlier crises in the early 1950s and late 1960s, is "best understood as part and parcel of a recurring pattern in the archipelago's post-independence history, wherein underlying tensions in Philippine society crystallized into full-blown political crises" (Hedman and Sidel 2000, 13). Wurfel (1988) saw it as part of a cycle of "development and decay."

The democratic transition that began after Marcos' fall in 1986 was only temporarily successful. Two more crises occurred in the following three decades. There was another "people power" style uprising, but this time against a freely and fairly elected president Joseph E. Estrada in 2001. His successor, Gloria Macapagal Arroyo, faced immediate and longer-term legitimation problems during her scandal-plagued tenure. In 2016, Duterte was elected promising on bloody "war on drugs.". Marcos, Jr., running with Duterte's daughter as his vice presidential candidate, easily won the 2022 presidential election assuring continuity with "Dutertismo" and invoking nostalgia for Marcos, Sr.'s authoritarian rule. This democratic backsliding occurred against the backdrop of "historically rooted structural conditions" in which neoliberal economic strategies restarted economic growth but failed to alleviate poverty significantly, allowing Duterte to secure power "on the back of the development failures of the past three decades" (Ramos 2021, 310). Cacique democracy had again proved unstable in the Philippines.

This explanation has the advantage of offering a plausible historical account that identifies recurring political problems traced back to severe structural inequalities in the Philippines. It is embedded in the continuing oligarchical character of the Philippine economy despite major transformations in its capitalist system away from dependence on agricultural commodities and a small industrial sector to a largely service-based economy with rampant property speculation (A. Raquiza 2018). While the dynamics of capitalist accumulation have changed, the "structural continuity" of a narrow Philippine oligarchy in the twentieth and early twenty-first centuries' Philippine history is striking (Rodan 2021, 242). Elections, which in the context of a huge gap between rich and poor are personality oriented with weak political parties lacking clear political programs, often fail to sufficiently "integrate" poor voters behind mainstream oligarchical candidates, allowing disruptive outsiders to win.

The Difference Philippine Presidents Make

As insightful as this structuralist perspective is, it does not offer an adequate account of agency. Of particular significance is the role of Philippine presidents in a "hyper-presidential system" (Rose-Ackerman and Desierto 2011). Duterte's drug war quickly undermined even the limited liberal constraints observed by his post-people power predecessors. By concentrating power during his elected presidency from 1966 and then by declaring martial law in 1972, Marcos broke the informal rules of the political game in the post-independence period, leading to the breakdown of a vibrant if flawed post-independence democracy (Thompson 1995, chp. 2). The precedent for aggrandizement had been set by Manuel L. Quezon as Commonwealth president from the mid-1930s who had called for "partyless" democracy, a euphemism for one-man rule (McCoy 1989). These strongmen presidents fashioned effective messaging to justify their concentration of power. They also often relied on political violence and instrumentalized the persistence of poverty as justification for their usurpation of power.

Yet other Philippine presidents have worked to restore or stabilize democracy after its collapse or severe decline, particularly Ramon Magsaysay (president from 1953 to 1957) and Cory Aquino (1986–92). Utilizing a liberal reformist discourse, they were supported by elite "strategic groups," particularly the Catholic Church hierarchy, big business leaders, civil society activists, and top military brass, sometimes with backing from the US government (Thompson 2010, 2014a).

Thus, alongside structural factors, the political strategies of key actors, particularly presidents and leaders of strategic groups, are of central importance. Oligarchical structures have both constrained and enabled presidential and elite group leadership in the Philippines, a process which in sociological theory has been termed "structuration" (Giddens 1984).[2] This Element employs

---

[2] It is beyond the scope of this Element to elaborate on Giddens' (1994) notion of structuration, influenced by Norbert Elias' earlier theory of "figuration" (van Krieken 2017). But it should be

such a structuration approach to analyze the country's recent reversion to strongman rule within the historical context of nearly a century of Philippine presidential politics. It also brings together three themes in the literature (patronage democracy, political violence, and widespread impoverishment) in an effort to provide a multifaceted account of the country's repeated democratic crises.

The Sections Ahead

Section 2 shows how the Philippines' extreme form of patronage-driven democracy has proved vulnerable to executive aggrandizement by transgressive presidents willing to violate prevailing norms and override weak formal institutional checks. Yet there has been pushback against this abuse of power by elite strategic groups, often backed by the US government, employing a discourse of liberal reformism. Strategic groups were key to the success of "people power" which led to the restoration of electoral democracy in 1986. But patronage dynamics resulted in repeated corruption scandals and undermined institution-building, discrediting the discourse of good governance and undermining elite guardianship. This created a political opportunity for a reversion to strongman rule while weakening elite pushback against it.

In order to understand the origins of Duterte's illiberal messaging, Section 3 examines the prevalence of localized political violence in the Philippines. By the mid-1980s, Davao City had become one of the most violent cities in the Philippines with communist rebels, anti-communist vigilantes, and the military as well as warlord politicians violently competing for power. As mayor, Duterte effectively triangulated between these forces, creating a neo-bossist model which proved appealing to voters given the weakness of state institutions in the Philippines, particularly a broken justice system. As president, Duterte nationalized this strategy, employing highly militarized "brute force governance" in his "war on drugs" and during the COVID-19 pandemic (Thompson 2022b). This also has historical parallels as Presidents Elpidio R. Quirino and Marcos, Sr., used local warlords and paramilitary groups to intimidate opponents, with Marcos also concentrating military powers under his direct control even before the declaration of martial law (Abueva 1971, 140; Berlin 1982). Reliance on political violence has been another hallmark of transgressive presidents.

---

noted that, for Giddens, agency is shaped by structures while structures themselves are conserved or transformed through the individuals' exercise of agency, with the interface being "structuration." Individuals or groups utilize structures to engage in social action but these "structures" are themselves the result of the very same social practices, leading Giddens to speak of the "duality of structure" (and, one should add, of agency as well).

Section 4 focuses on the political pattern of both decrying and deflecting from the country's highly unequal political economy. Repeated promises of land reform – from the US colonial era through the post–people power period – were broken. After declaring martial law in 1972, Marcos pledged to undertake mass-scale industrialization and extensive social, particularly land reform. Instead his "sultanistic" oligarchical rule ruined the economy and worsened social inequality. While presidents after the collapse of the dictatorship restored financial stability and catalyzed economic growth, they failed to eliminate mass poverty. "Proletarian populists" promising to help the majority of Filipinos who consider themselves poor were overthrown or cheated. This allowed Duterte to present himself as Filipinos' last hope, with his drug war deflecting from the real harm his brute force governance did to impoverished Filipinos.

After summarizing the overall argument, the conclusion briefly examines the causes and impact of Marcos, Jr.'s landslide victory in the 2022 presidential elections. It then considers whether the Philippines has now moved beyond the past pattern of cycling between democracy and autocratization.

2 Recurring Crises of Patronage Democracy

The Philippine presidency closely resembles Latin American "strong presidents" given the fiscal prerogatives and coercive powers of the chief executives of this Southeast Asian nation (Teehankee 2016, 294). Philippine presidents have much more formal power than their US counterparts, particularly given their wide discretion over budgetary matters, essential in a patronage-driven democracy, making them "patrons-in-chief" (Thompson 2014a; Holmes 2018; Teehankee and Calimbahin 2022). They can relegate the legislature, the courts, and independent bodies to subordinate status despite theoretically being coequal branches of government or constitutionally mandated agencies (Batalla, Romana, and Rodrigo 2018; Mendoza and Thompson 2018), meaning "the President's authority [is] nearly ubiquitous in the entire state apparatus" (Ronas 2016, 81).

Castañeda Anastacio (2016, preface; see also Webb 2017) argues that this "tyrannical potential" of Philippine presidents can be traced back to the American colonial era. During US rule in the early twentieth century, the "promise of America's liberal empire was negated by the imperative of insulating American authority from Filipino political demands," making the legacy of "constitutional autocracy as much American as it is Filipino" (Castañeda Anastacio 2016, preface).

Taking a comparative view, Rose-Ackerman and Desierto (2011) view the Philippines as one of the few cases globally of "hyper-presidentialism."

Bolongaita Jr. (1995, 110) has even argued that "among presidential democracies, the Philippine president virtually has no equal in terms of aggregate executive power."

Yet not all presidents have taken full advantage of the opportunity offered by a patronage-driven democracy to leverage weak checks and balances to consolidate their power beyond democratic bounds. One obvious example is Cory Aquino who, despite possessing extraordinary powers at the beginning of the presidency when she abolished the Marcos constitution and replaced local officials loyal to the fallen dictator, did not establish a dictatorship. Nor did she attempt to stay in power beyond the end of her term in 1992 despite ambiguity about whether the one-term limit set by the new constitution applied to her given the extra-constitutional circumstances of her rise to power (Thompson 2014a).

Before Duterte, two Philippine presidents were highly transgressive in making use of enormous executive powers while taking full advantage of the weakness of formal checks to severely weaken or overturn democracy. The first imperious Philippine chief executive was Commonwealth President Quezon (McCoy 1989). Quezon won a bitter factional battle – which ostensibly involved competing paths to independence – over his rival Sergio Osmeña. Quezon then easily triumphed with more than two-thirds of the vote in the country's first presidential elections of 1935 (running against the president of the First Philippine Republic until it fell to the US invader, Emilio Aguinaldo, who received less than 20 percent of the vote).

Building on his previous role as Senate president (1916–35), as Commonwealth President, Quezon was able to integrate patronage distribution from the local to national level, allowing constant "intervention and manipulation." Quezon claimed "90 percent" of his dealings with politicians involved patronage distribution (McCoy 2017, 13–14). Quezon reached the height of his power after his ruling party swept the 1941 legislative elections, with its leadership assenting to all of Quezon's handpicked senatorial candidates, including his bodyguard and purported pimp – an act which a Manila newspaper columnist compared to the Roman Emperor Caligula appointing his horse to the Roman Senate (cited in McCoy 2017, 124). All opposition senatorial bets were defeated (a feat not replicated until Duterte's allies did so in 2019). Through constitutional amendment, Quezon had decided to make Philippine senators elected nationally, uprooting them from their local political bases and making them more dependent on his patronage while extending his own term as president from six to eight years.

Quezon developed strongman messaging to match his patronage monopoly. He claimed the most appropriate political system in the country was a "partyless democracy," a politically convenient concept coined by political scientist Ricardo Pascual (Tigno 2018). In mid-1940, Quezon declared opposition parties and individual liberties to be democratic "fetishes" unsuitable to the Philippine context (McCoy 1989, 147). He marginalized the only remaining check on his power, the American High Commissioner, who in turn accused Quezon of trying to establish a dictatorship. Quezon had quickly veered toward one-man rule as it was "not in his nature to accept limitations on his power" (Abinales and Amoroso 2017, 153). As war approached, he gave himself additional emergency war powers but was forced to flee after the Japanese invasion, dying in exile in the United States two years later. Yet the precedent of the transformation of a competitive electoral system into one-man rule had been set.

Three decades later, Marcos followed Quezon's example. Even before he declared martial law in 1972, Marcos had become the most powerful president since independence in 1946 (Thompson 1995, chp. 2). Although costs of presidential campaigns had increased significantly before Marcos, with government overspending common during campaign years, Marcos ran deficits even in nonelection years to fund a huge infrastructure projects that were distributed to achieve maximum political advantage (Doronila 1985).

Under martial rule, elections were canceled, Congress abolished, the Supreme Court intimidated, and a new constitution put in place (through a pseudo referendum conducted by a show of hands in local barangays). Marcos was able to implement martial law with a limited amount of force as the opposition proved easy to buy off with promises of patronage, with the change in the distribution of largesse leading many previously anti-Marcos politicians to abandon their opposition activities and jockey for Marcos' goodwill instead (Thompson 1995, 63). Only a small group of self-exiled politicians (and allied activists) kept up opposition from abroad, attempting to compensate for the demobilization at home by contesting Marcos' international legitimacy in the United States and Europe (Shain and Thompson 1990; Sanchez 2017).

Marcos constructed an elaborate justification for martial law, not only in terms of threats posed by the far left (communists) and far right (oligarchs), but also by strongman messaging which promised fundamental social transformation to lessen poverty and injustice (discussed in Section 4) and political change. He claimed authoritarian rule was a necessary price for restoring order and accelerating development (Marcos 1974; Rosenberg 1979). Marcos imposed severe restrictions on a previously free (though factionalized and oligarchical) press, curbing opposition criticism of nepotism and favoritism.

Freed of electoral competition and media constraints, the Marcos martial law regime quickly become highly "sultanistic" in nature as the use of political authoritarianism was primarily directed toward private accumulation, with the proclaimed ideology of a "New Society" only providing a thin cover for kleptocracy (Thompson 1995, chp. 3, 1998; Winters 2011, chp. 4). As Linz (2000 [1975], 152) has argued, the neo-Weberian term "sultanism" character-izes the "personalistic and particularistic use of power for essentially private ends of the ruler" who makes "the country essentially like a huge domain." This blurs the "boundaries between the public treasury and the private wealth of the ruler." Marcos and his wife Imelda became the richest couple in the Philippines and among the wealthiest in the world. Primitivo Mijares (1976), an early defector from the regime – who apparently paid for his disloyalty with his life – famously termed it a "conjugal dictatorship." Highly personalistic dicta-torships are particularly vulnerable to "tell-all" accounts by disaffected former insiders (Thompson 1998). Mijares, Marcos' former chief media propagandist and once close adviser, exposed not just Marcos and his wife's personal foibles and abuse of power but also demonstrated how corruption constituted *the very form of rule itself.* "Crony capitalism," a term coined by a journalist writing about the Marcos regime in 1980, soon came to inform the global study of kleptocracy (Hau 2016).

Checking Transgressive Presidents

But Philippine presidents since Quezon have not been able to transgress against the rules of the Philippines' competitive electoral game of politics at will. Since the early 1950s, two powerful extra-institutional checks on presidential powers have been created to constrain would-be imperious chief executives: a political discourse of "liberal reformism" and elite "strategic group" veto actors (Thompson 2014b). Despite the prevalence of patronage politics and the cor-responding weakness of political ideologies in the Philippines, presidential and other political candidates in the Philippines have long crafted campaign narra-tives to appeal to the hopes and values of the electorate, forging an emotional link between voters and candidates. While not programmatic in a systematic sense, political narratives in the Philippine context do have an ideological quality in that they present an oversimplified and one-sided view of reality, which can be used to disguise class or other interests (Thompson 2010; Teehankee 2016).

Given the prevalence of scandal and a tendency toward autocracy in a patronage-dominated democracy, a common narrative by opposition candi-dates has been one of liberal reformism which stresses the need to protect civil liberties and safeguard fair elections while promoting "good governance." This narrative can be traced back to Jose Rizal, a Philippine national hero who was a novelist, eye doctor, linguist, and historian, among other talents. His novel *Noli Me Tangere*, published in 1887, sarcastically attacked "untouchable" corruption under Spanish rule (Claudio 2019, chp. 3). Another precedent-setter was Juan M. Sumulong, the maternal grandfather of Cory Aquino, who was known as the "Great Dissenter" and "Brains of the Opposition" for his criticism of abuses by US colonial officials and of Quezon's senate and Commonwealth presidencies (Guerrero 1938; National Historical Institute 1990).

Given the fact that most of the population of the Philippines is still poor and relatively powerless, elite strategic groups in the Philippines are more hegemonic than the "power elite" in the United States (Mills 1956). For Evers (1973; also Evers, Schiel, and Korff 1988; Berner 2001; Evers and Gerke 2008), strategic groups in Southeast Asia are not reducible to a social class (e.g., the bourgeoisie) that form a homogenous ruling elite. As group consciousness emerges, heterogeneous elite groups begin to act strategically to accumulate power resources and to influence state policy. Although possessing distinct resources (top military brass: coercion; big business: capital/property; religious leaders: a belief system; civil society activists: foreign networks/salient issues), these groups unite around a program of political action based on overlapping interests and ideological commitments. Going beyond the general oligarchical domination perspective discussed in the Introduction, a strategic group approach offers the advantage of analyzing particular elite leaders whose backing is crucial for a stable presidency, but whose withdrawal of support can weaken presidents or even lead to their downfall. As extra-electoral power brokers, strategic groups can buttress or challenge the enormous power of presidents.

Four extra-electoral strategic groups have played critical roles in constraining presidential power since independence in 1946, during the latter stages of the Marcos dictatorship, and in the post–people power period – the Catholic Church hierarchy, big business leaders, civil society activists, and top military brass. Except for the military, these groups are officially outside of government, although they all have close ties to the state, with representatives of big business and civil society groups often taking high-ranking positions in presidential cabinets. They all have large organizations that allow them to mobilize supporters for or against a president, either nonviolently (e.g., through demonstrations) or with a show of force (by military intervention). In addition, the US government has sometimes backed these groups as part of its general interference in Philippine politics. However, as elsewhere, the United States has often fallen far short of its pro-democracy rhetoric, as its long-term support for the Marcos dictatorship indicated (Bonner 1987).

To turn from these powerful strategic groups to the Philippines' weak party system, during the postindependence, pre-martial law era (1946–72), two major political parties, the *Nacionalistas* and the Liberals, regularly alternated in power. A major reason for this turnover is that over time there were increasing numbers of defectors from the incumbent party's presidential administration who felt shortchanged in all-important patronage distribution. But the success of this defection strategy depended on the ruling party's obedience to an informal set of political rules that kept country's politics competitive. It was not abstract constitutional principles or civil liberties that were scrupulously upheld or that limits on campaign spending were strictly enforced. Rather it was the lively (if largely elite-controlled) media, some degree of parity in electoral spending, a balance of election-related violence, and fair refereeing by the Commission on Elections (COMELEC) that were crucial (Thompson 1995, chp. 1).

But when these informal rules were threatened, the survival of Philippine democracy was at stake. Electoral democracy almost broke down just three years after independence in the 1949 presidential election in which the Liberal incumbent Elpidio R. Quirino (who had succeeded president Manuel A. Roxas after he had died suddenly in 1948) was elected. Quirino was accused of turning the polls into the "most fraudulent and terroristic" election the country had ever experienced (Thompson 1995, 24). Terror was employed by pro-Quirino goons, election officials were bribed, voter lists padded, and electoral fraud widespread. Campaign overspending by Quirino's government plunged the country into a foreign exchange crisis. This political crisis added to worries that the "bullets not ballots" slogan of a growing pro-communist Huk insurgency might ultimately prevail, discussed further in the next section.

Against this context of manipulated elections and communist mobilization, the US government, and its Central Intelligence Agency (CIA) in particular, provided assistance to the organizing of the National Movement for Free Elections (NAMFREL), with the catchphrase "protect the ballot and save the nation" (Hedman 2006). Supported by groups linked to the Catholic Church, big business, and civil society, NAMFREL aimed to limit electoral fraud and violence in the next presidential election in 1953. This bolstered the prospects of the opposition *Nacionalista* Party's presidential candidate, former Secretary of Defense Ramon Magsaysay, who was close to the US Air Force officer and later CIA operative Col. Edward G. Lansdale (Lansdale 1972). Through effective messaging aided by friendly US media, Magsaysay's honesty was contrasted with Quirino's corruption and "moral weakness," which the *Nacionalistas* referred to as their "great crusade" to save the country (Thompson 1995, 27–28). Anticipating Quirino would spend heavily using government funds, rely on local bosses, and engage in fraud to win reelection, Magsaysay organized elite volunteers and appealed to voters directly through an unprecedented barnstorming campaign that took him to some of the remotest parts of the archipelago. Nicknamed "the Guy," Magsaysay called himself a "man of the people" with his large rallies known as the "Magsaysay boom" (Thompson 1995, 28). The Catholic Church hierarchy came out in open support of NAMFREL's electoral watchdog effort. The US government helped fund Magsaysay's campaign. Several of its naval vessels entered Manila Bay shortly before the election in a kind of anti-fraud gunboat diplomacy. With sympathetic officers in the Philippine military ready to back Magsaysay's claim to power in the case of electoral fraud, Quirino was defeated in a landslide in which Magsaysay won nearly 70 percent of the vote.

About two decades later, however, a similar elite coalition failed to stop Marcos from declaring martial law. Like Quirino in 1949, Marcos' use of coercion (discussed in the next section) led to opposition outrage and electoral overspending in 1969 resulted in economic crisis. In response, the traditional political opposition resorted to extreme tactics, supporting student demonstrations, launching a failed assassination plot, and working together with both communist rebels (with opposition senator Benigno "Ninoy" S. Aquino, Jr. even helping the Maoist Communist Party of the Philippines found an army in 1968) and Muslim secessionist groups (Corpus 1989; Thompson 1995, chp. 2; Scalice 2017). After performing well in the 1971 election, the opposition seemed poised to regain the presidency in 1973 when Marcos was barred from seeking another term. But instead of deterring martial law, the opposition's extremism contributed to the political polarization which Marcos seized upon to rationalize the need for dictatorship. Marcos also consolidated control over the military, carefully courted US support at the time of the Vietnam war, and won over big business with promises of a comprehensive development strategy.

But a little over a decade later, the mainstream opposition was able to restart its campaign against Marcos. Most wealthy capitalists and executives of major companies had embraced martial law as they hoped the Philippines would become another Asia "tiger" economy such as South Korea. Yet a few businessmen joined a brief arson campaign against the Marcos regime and there was also growing discontent after a financial scandal in 1981 revealed the degree of cronyism in the regime. But it was not until the assassination of opposition leader Ninoy Aquino, Jr. in 1983 and the resulting economic crisis and moral outrage generated by the murder that large demonstrations against the Marcos regime in business district Makati (the "confetti revolution") began (Thompson 1995, chp. 7; Evangelista 2015).

Only seventeen of the country's more than 100 Catholic bishops had openly criticized Marcos during much of his dictatorship, opting instead for an ostensible strategy of "critical collaboration" espoused by Cardinal Sin, leader of the Catholic Bishops' Conference of the Philippines (CBCP) that emphasized the latter with little of the former (Thompson 1995, 118). Yet there was activism elsewhere in the church exemplified by Mariani C. Dimaranan, known as Sister Mariani, a Catholic nun and activist who ran the Task Force Detainees of the Philippines (TFDP). Established shortly after martial law, TFDP documented human rights abuses by the regime and supported human rights defenders (Sanchez 2017). It was only after the shock of the Aquino assassination that the church hierarchy began to regularly criticize the regime. Cardinal Sin and other leading Church officials openly embraced "conservative Church reformism," which shared with its big business allies the goals of ending arbitrary repression and extreme corruption. But it put little focus on the failures of development or lack of social reform (Barry 2006).

Closely linked to the Catholic Church, some opposition politicians and, to a lesser extent, business oppositionists were social democrat activists. Many of these groups traced their roots to the protest-filled period from Marcos' controversial reelection in 1969 to the declaration of martial law in 1972. But wary of communist activists (who, in turn, were suspicious of "Socdems" with close Church ties), social democrats had created a separate political identity. Largely demobilized by repression and fear during the early dictatorship, they returned to activism in collaboration with opposition politicians' campaigns in the 1978 polls in Metro Manila. But all opposition candidates in the capital city were defeated in a fraudulent election, and several were detained. The Socdems, following the example of a failed arson campaign led by a few businessmen backed by some Jesuit church leaders, opted for a terrorist campaign. This had little impact aside from one bomb attack on a visiting tourist convention that led to some bad publicity for the regime but the jailing of key activists. Another Socdem faction, engaged in an ill-fated attempt to create an opposition army in cooperation with the Moro secessionists with support from Malaysian authorities (nursing a grudge over a territorial dispute) in Sabah. This effort also came to nothing, with its ringleaders arrested. But after the Aquino assassination, social democratic activists with close Church ties played a key organizational role in the anti-Marcos protests (Thompson 1995, chp. 5).

The Aquino Assassination and People Power

But it was not the "sultanization" and brutality of the Marcos regime alone that triggered the rise of the noncommunist, and now "moderate" opposition that professed belief in nonviolence.[3] Rather, it was that "one of their own" in the figure of an elite politician Ninoy Aquino had been targeted. The Marcos government estimated 165 rallies, marches, and other demonstrations took place in the first five weeks after the assassination alone (Thompson 1995, 116). Observers began noticing that it was no longer radical activists who made up the majority of those attending. Many of the protesters now came from the "middle forces" defined as "formerly apolitical middle-class and upper-class groups that joined the struggle mostly after the assassination of Ninoy Aquino" (Claudio 2013, 60).

The Ninoy Aquino Foundation held an exhibition on Aquino's life in Makati. It displayed Aquino's possessions like the relics of saints and the bloodied shirt and themes of martyrdom were reminiscent of the museum display in Fort Santiago about national hero Jose Rizal's execution in 1896. Ileto (1985, 12) has argued that the assassination appeared to most Filipinos to be a "familiar drama involving familiar themes," with Aquino compared to Rizal and, like the national hero, sometimes even portrayed as a Filipino Christ. When Marcos denied responsibility for the assassination, a common rejoinder was "Pontius Pilate" (Ileto 1985, 12). The emotions of the moment were captured by the journalist Ninez Cacho-Olivares who wrote that because Aquino was a politician "he may not have had the interest of the Filipino at heart." But when "I looked at his ashen face, the bullet wound, and the blood all over his shirt . . . I said to myself . . . I have no more doubts. You loved your country and your people. God be with you, always, wherever you may be" (cited in Thompson 1995, 116).

Later in her campaign for the presidency during the February 1986 "snap" presidential elections, Cory Aquino would simply recount what she and her husband had suffered at the hands of Marcos. The author and many others noted that despite her unschooled, monotone delivery, her speech deeply moved the huge crowds that turned out during her campaign as her husband's murder and her campaign for justice symbolized the moral nature of the struggle against Marcos (Thompson 1995, chp. 8).

Alternative print and radio media (backed by the big business leaders and the Catholic Church hierarchy) emerged after the Aquino assassination, helping circumvent a sanitized mainstream media. With Marcos unwilling to resign or arrange a transition to democracy (as rulers of more institutionalized military regimes had done in many South American countries, for example), many opposition politicians decided to participate in legislative elections in mid-1984 despite Marcos' past record of electoral manipulation. Although there was

---

[3] The traditional opposition's shift toward a nonviolent strategy was influenced by Ninoy Aquino's enthusiasm for Richard Attenborough's 1982 movie *Gandhi* (Thompson 1995, 112).

extensive cheating, a surprising number of opposition candidates still won, giving them a psychological boost even though their power as a minority in the National Assembly was limited. Marcos – under pressure from the United States, continued protests, and ongoing economic woes – in an interview on US TV announced a "snap" presidential election in February 1986. All major national opposition groups except the communists (who had failed to create an alliance with social democrats a half year earlier) decided to participate.

But when Marcos abruptly called elections, the opposition had not yet agreed on a common presidential candidate despite efforts by a "convenor group" made up of senior opposition figures to do so. Under pressure from the Catholic Church hierarchy and big business leaders, Salvador "Doy" R. H. Laurel (a son of Jose Laurel, president during the Japanese occupation and defeated presidential candidate in 1949 who allied with Magsaysay in 1953) agreed to slide down to the vice presidency. Despite Laurel being the leader of the largest opposition political coalition, a consensus emerged that Aquino, as the widow of the opposition martyr Aquino, had more "moral capital" (Kane 2009). Like many dynastic female leaders in Asia (such as Myanmar's Aung San Suu Kyi or Sri Lanka's Chandrika Kumaratunga) who inherited the charisma of their martyred father or husbands, Cory was seen as selfless, not caught up in the Machiavellian struggles of male politicians (Thompson 2007).

In a new incarnation officially called the National Citizens Movement for Free Elections (NAMFREL), it monitored the polling and produced an independent vote count claiming Aquino had won the election despite an official count showing she had lost. Marcos' apparent electoral manipulation embittered an imagined community of robbed voters who could easily be mobilized against the regime (Kuntz and Thompson 2009).

The people power insurrection that ousted Marcos was sparked by the attempt to hunt down military rebels angered by Marcos' personalization of the military. Facing annihilation by government soldiers and tanks, Cardinal Sin played a key role in getting hundreds of thousands of Manileños to rally around their positions to protect them from attack. After a four-day standoff, Marcos fled the Philippines in a helicopter provided by the United States (he later claimed to have been kidnapped). With Cory Aquino sworn into office on the last day of the uprising, the victory of the forces behind people's power seemed complete.

The Disjunction of Liberal Reformism and the Rise of Illiberal Democracy

Philippine electoral democracy appeared to consolidate gradually after the first turbulent years following Marcos' overthrow. The breakup of the fragile coalition between politicians and activists loyal to President Cory Aquino and those linked to Laurel as well as military rebels tied to Juan Ponce Enrile destabilized the new government. The result was nine coup attempts: one was tellingly dubbed "God Save the Queen," indicating they had expected Cory Aquino to reign, not actually rule (Thompson 2007). Aquino's administration survived in part due to US backing as it moved to the right on security, human rights, and social issues. It also relied heavily on the new Chief of Staff of the Armed Forces and later Secretary of Defense, Fidel V. Ramos (who died in August 2022), to reunite the military in support of civilian rule. The legislative elections of 1987, though marred by violence and dominated by dynastic politics, were largely free and fair, luring politicians of all different stripes – including Marcos loyalists – back into the electoral arena. Although Ramos won the 1992 presidential elections by the narrowest of margins with fewer than a quarter of the votes, he managed to end military rebellions and calm the country politically.

Skipping ahead to the administration of Noynoy Aquino (2010–16), economic acceleration that began under his predecessor Gloria Macapagal Arroyo (2001–10) continued but without mass demonstrations and coup attempts that had marred her legitimacy-challenged presidency. Noynoy Aquino, widely seen as personally honest, promised to take the "straight path" (*daang matuwid*) to clean up corruption which he claimed would also eradicate poverty. Under Aquino, economic growth was among the highest in the Association of Southeast Asian (ASEAN) nations. Some high-ranking officials accused of corruption, including the supreme court chief justice, were removed. More people paid their taxes after a Bureau of International Revenue crackdown. International credit ratings agencies upped the Philippines' rating to investment grade while its ranking in Transparency International's Corruption Perception Index improved. Aquino seemed to be moving fast along the "straight path" (Thompson 2014b).

Why then did electoral democracy in the Philippines prove vulnerable to Duterte's democratic backsliding?[4] The liberal reformist discourse had come to appear uncaring and morally self-righteous as poverty rates and unemployment remained high during the post-Marcos era (discussed in Section 4). In addition, several scandals, many concerning smuggling, were damaging to the second Aquino administration's "good governance"

---

[4] There are several indices measuring democratic backsliding – "state-led debilitation or elimination of any of the political institutions that sustain an existing democracy" (Bermeo 2016, 5). Data from the Varieties of Democracy project, arguably the most comprehensive, show both civil liberties and liberal democratic measures declined substantially under Duterte (www.v-dem.net/data_analysis/CountryGraph/).

narrative. What caused particular outrage (and led to large protests) were revelations about abuse of the Priority Development Assistance Fund (PDAF), the main vehicle for government political pork barreling (Holmes 2018). It was revealed that doling out patronage to legislators had been crucial to passing reformist legislation or to remove supposedly corrupt officials (Tiglao 2013). Funds often ended up in legislators' pockets instead of going to public works projects. Opposition legislators were targeted in the follow-up investigation, raising suspicions Aquino was using the scandal as a chance to strike back at political enemies rather than make a serious effort to eliminate abuses. Given the weakness of political parties and lack of ideological commitment to major policy reforms, pork barreling was the chief tool at the disposal of Noynoy Aquino, as earlier presidents, to pass their legislative agenda, including major reforms (Holmes 2018). Caught up in scandal seemingly unavoidable in a patronage-driven system, Aquino's "straight path" had reached a dead end (Thompson 2014b).

Patronage politics also undermined institution-building. The country's bureaucracy has a checkered history due to political interference and corrupt practices (Hodder 2018). Despite reforms made after Marcos fell from power, career civil servants continued frequently to complain that "what seems to matter is an ability to manoeuvre through a well-entrenched system of patronage" (Hodder 2018, 76). Corruption in the courts was perceived to be particularly widespread. Offering his drug crackdown his silver bullet (as discussed in detail in the next section), Duterte played to a "legally cynical public" that did not trust a broken judicial system to convict drug offenders whose cases were often dismissed on technicalities, with accusations it was far too easy to bribe judges and otherwise manipulate the courts (Narag 2017). This led many Filipinos to "cheer" Duterte, a former prosecutor, who called for "the sidestepping of due process and human rights of the suspects, with the belief that we need to cleanse first the corrupt legal system before we can even introduce any meaningful reforms" (Narag 2017).

Duterte's effective strongman messaging made him less dependent on vote buying and clientelist networks. Despite receiving funding from a former Marcos crony and from the Marcoses themselves, election observers reported Duterte had considerably less campaign "machinery" than his key presidential rival, the Aquino administration-backed Mar Roxas (Tiglao 2016; Vitug 2016). Instead, Duterte's strong anti-drug narrative and the lack of popular enthusiasm for Roxas' standard reformist appeals proved crucial to Duterte's victory. Duterte's allies then swept the 2019 mid-term elections less due to "the systematic mobilization of patronage" by the government which Duterte did not prioritize, than to his popularity as a strongman (Kasuya and Teehankee 2020, 112–114).[5]

The rise of Duterte's violent populism was also facilitated by the weakening of key elite strategic groups. The Catholic Church hierarchy became politicized during the late period of Marcos' rule, taking on a self-anointed role as "guardian of democracy" (Barry 2006). But increasingly fragmented leadership among the bishops and revelations of sexual abuses weakened the church's standing as did its adamant opposition to public provision of contraception provided by a reproductive health bill passed in 2012 (Rufo 2013; Dañguilan 2018). Duterte easily outmaneuvered the church by threatening to expose its sex scandals, claiming as a child he had been abused by a priest (*Reuters*, October 11, 2016). Archbishop Socrates Villegas, President of CBCP, initially called for "vigilant collaboration" with the Duterte administration, reminiscent of the church's official stance of "critical collaboration" early in the Marcos dictatorship (Williams 2018). Although the church's leadership later became Duterte's "fiercest foes" (Coronel 2017), they had already become politically marginalized.

With Duterte's election, Socdem and breakaway "Natdem" civil society activists (particularly *Akbayan*, the Citizens' Action Party) who had played a central role in the Aquino administration, found they were sharing the blame for its failings. Although civil society groups organized several major protests against Duterte's drug war which put the administration under pressure, they could not be sustained (Thompson 2021).

Duterte did not fear "to transgress liberal discourse" which did not only "not trouble a significant part of the population, they've even clapped for it" (Bello 2016). He quickly elevated the role of the Philippine National Police, bringing in his former Davao police chief Ronald "Bato" M. dela Rosa as its new head, effectively making the police a new strategic group. Under Duterte, the police were "given extensive powers to amplify the state's power" in the brutal war on drugs, during the strict and lengthy lockdowns during the COVID-19 pandemic, and to enforce a contentious anti-terrorism law, securitizing these campaigns "to bolster an illiberal regime" (Agojo 2021, 363).

---

[5] Although patronage is crucial to the exercise of presidential power in the Philippines, particularly through the control of Congress, its importance in national election campaigns is declining and may have been overestimated in the past (Teehankee 2016). Even an influential advocate of the patron–client model, Landé (1996, 107) later revised his position, acknowledging local political "leaders can no longer deliver their constituents blindly" to national candidates in exchange for patronage. In presidential elections since people power, Ramos was elected, albeit extremely narrowly, as Cory Aquino's chosen successor in 1992 and Gloria Macapagal Arroyo "won" in the highly controversial 2004 polls she was accused of manipulating. But "outsider" candidates not endorsed by incumbents, such as Duterte in 2016 and Estrada in 1998, have also triumphed despite having fewer patronage resources.

Residual institutional barriers were quickly sidelined, giving rise to an illiberal democracy (Dressel and Bonoan 2019; Thompson 2019; Curato 2021; Fernandez 2021). Inevitable patronage-driven defections gave his allies control over the lower house despite Duterte belonging to a micro-party with only a handful of seats (he later sidelined the party, the once progressive and anti-Marcos PDP-Laban). The defection of most members of the former ruling Liberal Party to Duterte's coalition showed how hollow its promise under Noynoy Aquino had been to become "programmatic" with a clear political doctrine and membership loyalty despite the former president's warnings about Duterte's illiberalism. It proved to be just as much a party of patronage-dependent *"trapos"* (traditional politicians) as every other. The courts proved reluctant to interfere with Duterte's drug war, even after he had produced (without evidence) a list of judges supposedly involved in the illegal narcotics trade. An independent agency, the Commission on Human Rights, documented the drug war killings but had no enforcement powers to stop them and was nearly defunded by Duterte's allies in Congress.

Duterte was an unrepentantly misogynist president whose repeated rape jokes brought him international notoriety but have been widely interpreted in the Philippines as rejecting the hypocritical moralism of the Aquino administration in favor of a "crass" but more authentic politics (Curato and Ong 2018). It is telling that four of the highest-profile opposition figures Duterte has targeted have been women. Duterte jailed senator Leila de Lima who had previously chaired the Commission on Human Rights and had been justice secretary. She had investigated Duterte's involvement in drug vigilante killings when he was mayor of Davao. As senator she chaired senate hearings examining Duterte's Davao-based and now national drug war killings before being removed by the president's allies in the autumn of 2016. They then interrogated De Lima's driver, who was also her lover (a dual sin in a class-bound society with double standards), in order to "slut shame" her and "prove" alleged links between de Lima and drug lords. Duterte fired Vice President Maria Leonor "Leni" Robredo from a cabinet post after she criticized the drug war. Maria Ressa, CEO of the influential online newspaper *Rappler* which has been highly critical of Duterte who later was cowinner of the Nobel Peace Prize for her critical journalism, still faces fifteen years in jail based on cases supported by the Duterte administration widely seen as harassment and part of a general effort to intimidate critical voices in the media (Crispin 2018). Former supreme court chief justice Maria Lourdes Sereno was removed from office through a highly irregular legal maneuver after questioning Duterte's claim several judges were involved in the drug trade (Deinla, Taylor, and Rood 2018).

Conclusion

This section explored how patronage-driven democracy facilitated executive aggrandizement by three transgressive presidents – Quezon, Marcos, and Duterte – who used strongman messaging as they overrode weak formal democratic checks. It also analyzed the stronger but uncertain informal constraints imposed on presidential power by elite strategic groups employing a liberal reformist discourse. This first occurred after the manipulated 1949 presidential elections and led to Magsaysay's victory four years later. But such an effort two decades later failed to stop Marcos' march to martial law. Yet Marcos was later overthrown by people power with a similar elite "hegemonic bloc" at the forefront. After Marcos' fall, corruption scandals, seemingly inevitable in a patronage-dominated system, belied the promise to restore "good governance" and also discredited the elite strategic groups promoting it. With reformism and elite guardianship weakened, a political opportunity for Duterte's highly illiberal messaging emerged.

3 Nationalizing Localized Political Violence

As discussed in the Introduction and previous section, Duterte quickly regressed Philippine democracy after winning the presidency in 2016. To understand the lineages of his illiberalism, the types and prevalence of localized political violence are first surveyed. Next, the Davao City context – which became an epicenter of rebellion, anti-insurgency campaigns, and warlordism – is examined as this was where Duterte's "neo-bossism" was birthed. Having effectively securitized the danger posed by illegal drugs as mayor, Duterte then made his promise to carry out a "war on drugs" throughout the Philippines his primary presidential campaign theme and his signature program as president. Duterte was thus an innovator in political violence. His nationalization of this model fundamentally transformed Philippine politics by making violent populism appealing to the majority of Filipinos (Thompson 2022a).

Three Forms of Political Violence

Three kinds of political violence have bedeviled the country's local politics since the Commonwealth era, accelerating after independence, and then growing exponentially during the late Marcos and post–people power periods: rebellion (chiefly by communist insurgents and Muslim secessionists), anti-insurgency campaigns (conducted by the Philippine military and vigilante groups) and bossism (particularly between competing warlords) (Reyes 2016, 2022; Iglesias 2018). While these forms of violence can be distinguished ideal typically, in reality they have often overlapped, intersected, and reinforced one another. The military has fought rebels but repression has often led to more rebellion; political bosses, while regularly involved in the military's anti-insurgency campaigns, have also occasionally worked together with insurgents; former communists have sometimes joined anti-communist militias; occasionally military officers have defected to the insurgents.

Insurgencies justified by extreme social inequality have a long history in the Philippines. By some estimates, the New People's Army of the Communist Party of the Philippines (CPP-NPA) has been waging, since 1968, Asia's longest-running insurgency, costing up to 40,000 rebels', soldiers', and civilians' lives (Robles 2019). But already in the early twentieth century, several small millenarian movements agitating against landlord abuses were joined by "secular" insurgents, often assisted by veterans of the Philippine–American War, in smaller-scale rebellions during the early American colonial period (Abinales and Amoroso 2017, 147). By the 1930s, both the Partido Komunista ng Pilipinas (Philippine Communist Party or PKP) which focused on organizing workers, and the Sakdals (meaning "to accuse" in an apparent reference to Zola's *J'accuse* open letter in response to the Dreyfus Affair), which called for comprehensive rural and urban reforms, were active (Terami-Wada 1988, 133). The PKP grew during the Second World War when it played a key role in the popular front against the Japanese and then provided leadership of the Hukalahap (known as the Huk) rebellion which grew rapidly in the early 1950s (Quimpo 2008, 55). The establishment of the CPP as a breakaway faction from the PKP in 1968 was a delayed "expression of the Sino-Soviet split in global Stalinism" (Scalice 2017, 1; see also Weekley 2001). While the PKP moved to collaborate with Marcos, who at the time was pursuing closer relations with the Soviet Union, the CPP allied with several leading anti-Marcos politicians/warlords (most notably opposition leader Ninoy Aquino, Jr.) and launched a new armed struggle in the countryside (Jones 1989, 27–30; Scalice 2017, 378).

A major rebellion in Sulu province by the Moro National Liberation Movement (MNLF), an alliance of Muslim student activists and anti-Marcos Muslim warlord politicians, began in western Mindanao directly after martial law was declared and continued through the mid-1970s (McKenna 1998, chp. 7). The city of Jolo was largely destroyed in a major battle in 1974, with thousands reportedly killed in the conflict until a ceasefire was reached in 1976 (Stauffer 1981; McKenna 1998, chp. 7). Despite the military tripling in size after martial law, the Moro war diverted much of the armed force's attention, costing the regime billions of dollars while its concentration of forces near Manila to protect Marcos further sapped military resources available to conduct an anti-insurgency effort against communist rebels (Thompson 1995, 99; McKenna 1998, chp. 7; Institute for Autonomy and Development 2015).

This helped the CPP-NPA grow from a small Maoist breakaway faction that had been expelled from the PKP in the late 1960s to an army of over 20,000 by the early 1980s, concentrated in deprived rural areas in the country. Similar to warnings against the growth of the PKP-Huk rebellion, US analysts in the early 1980s began warning of a communist takeover in the Philippines by Maoist insurgents (Munro 1985).

Aside from the CPP-NPA's flexible military strategy and growing combat experience, the highly personalist character of the Marcos regime aided the rebels, with arbitrary state repression and land grabbing further fueling discontent (Thompson 1995, chp. 5). The CPP also turned to urban areas, using united fronts to launch general strikes (*Welgang Bayan*) "aimed at shutting down the Mindanao economy and creating political havoc" in order "to paralyze the economic, political, and social machinery of the dictatorship . . . and facilitate its downfall" (Munro 1985). They also formed sparrow units to gun down "unpopular government officials and security personnel at will" (Vartavarian 2019a). Although later officially disavowing this urban insurrectionist "Sandinista-Paradigm" (named after the Sandinista rebels' successful urban-based revolution in Nicaragua in 1979), the CPP leadership was tapping into a strong sense of exploitation by workers and squatters in urban areas to up the revolutionary ante (Collier 1995).

Often brutal counterinsurgency tactics were used by the military and paramilitary groups against insurgents. The mid-1935 *Sakdal* revolt near Manila provided the American colonial government with an opportunity to repress them as well as the PKP (Abinales and Amoroso 2017, 148–149). Presenting himself as the guarantor of political stability and pledging greater justice, Manuel Quezon won the presidential election later that year with the slogan "Quezon or chaos" while promising major social policy reforms, a pledge he left largely unfulfilled as discussed in the next section (Abinales and Amoroso 2017, 149). The anti-Japanese Huk rebels had tried but failed to negotiate with the Americans after the war, to whom anti-communism was more important than the common anti-Japanese cause during the Second World War (Kerkvliet 1977). With the PKP and their Huk allies seeking to become a legal political movement, they ran progressive congressional candidates in the 1946 elections. But all their winning candidates were expelled on dubious grounds from Congress in order for the Philippine government to be able to pass a controversial trade parity agreement with the United States. (Jimenez 2020). With state repression ratcheting up, the PKP-led Huks returned to armed insurgency. Besides a more effective counterinsurgency strategy supported by the United States, the tide against the rebellion turned in no small part due to the same motley crew of Jesuits, social democrats, military officers, and spies discussed in the previous section that worked to get former Secretary of Defense Ramon Magsaysay elected in 1953 as the "savior of democracy" from the communist threat.

Military counterinsurgency during the Marcos martial law period often targeted civilians suspected of communist sympathies, with entire villages sometimes burned in a manner parallel to the Vietnam war (to which the Philippines had briefly contributed troops to the American military campaign there). The Task Force of Detainees estimated during the Marcos dictatorship over 3,000 suspected communist sympathizers were killed with tens of thousands arrested, many of them tortured by military units that became notorious for committing rights abuses (McCoy 2001). When NPA "sparrows" began assassinating military personnel beginning in the early 1980s, the Armed Forces of the Philippines (AFP) units responded with targeted crackdowns on urban areas, abductions, and killings, often of those accused of collaborating with the communists but not combatants themselves. But rather than defeat the insurgency, outrage at military repression strengthened it in the late Marcos era (Mediansky 1986).

Governments after people power continued to give the military carte blanche to target rebellious workers and peasants as well as lawyers and other human rights advocates who they claimed were allied with the communists. In fact, the legitimacy enjoyed by the national government after the restoration of electoral democracy helped justify such repression against "enemies of the state" (Reyes 2022). Although he initially attempted to negotiate a peace settlement with the CPP as president, Duterte later stepped up anti-insurgency efforts, passing an "anti-terrorism" law that critics said would lead to the targeting of legal leftists (Mendoza and Romano 2020). In addition, the military had long informally relied on vigilantes to fight communists. van der Kroef (1988) counted more than 200 groups organized shortly before and immediately after Marcos' fall from power.

A third form of political violence prevalent in local politics is coercion employed by political warlords or bosses (Reyes 2022). Sidel (1999) understands bossism as involving coercive control over territory and local populations. This has often led to violent feuds between local strongmen and their political rivals. Confined to the lowest rung on the political ladder during the Spanish rule, local elite power increased under US colonialism, leading to the "emergence and entrenchment of small-town bosses, provincial 'warlords,' and authoritarian presidents by providing mechanisms for private monopolization of resources and prerogatives of the state" (Sidel 1999, 19). Although there was much continuity between the US colonial and independence state, the Second World War led to the rise of a new kind of political strongman, often of lower-class origins, who had morphed from anti-Japanese guerillas into local warlords and benefited from US patronage and reparations paid after the war (Abinales and Amoroso 2017, 189). They tended to gravitate to the newly founded Liberal Party which won presidential elections in 1946 and, controversially, in 1949 (as discussed in the previous section). Local strongmen also helped the military repress the Huk rebels.

Most local bosses became less active after the declaration of martial law, although the marginalization of several key local strongmen in Muslim Mindanao was a trigger for the Moro war during the early dictatorship period (McKenna 1998, chp. 7). Bossism made a violent reappearance in the country's local politics in the two elections held by Marcos after the Aquino assassination in 1983. A huge protest movement led Marcos to allow semi-competitive elections as an escape valve for popular grievances. This made coercion an increasingly valuable electoral tool (even more so when elections became largely free if not entirely fair after the dictator's fall in 1986). Violence worsened when competition between local bosses who built up powerful "private armies" was particularly intense, sometimes requiring intervention by the national state (Rimban 2011). Voters were often intimidated, ballot boxes stuffed, and, in extreme cases, "no opposition" elections took place, with only a single candidate running as all challengers had been sufficiently intimidated (Arguillas 2011, 12–14). In the 1984 legislative assembly elections, there were a reported 348 election-related killings, making it more violent than any pre-martial law poll, with warlords belonging almost exclusively to the pro-Marcos camp. Strong-arming local politicians were active in most provinces and even in the business district of Makati in Metro Manila (Thompson 1995, 126). Warlord violence continued during the "snap" presidential elections two years later in which 264 were reported killed. In one of the most gruesome incidents during the presidential campaign, a former governor and opposition activist, Evelio Javier, was assassinated in broad daylight on the front steps of the capital of Antique province by hired guns of local warlord Arturo Pacificador (Thompson 1995, 142).

After the collapse of the dictatorship, national elites "easily reconnected with sub-national strongmen." But with the "regional crony plenipotentiaries" – particularly those who controlled key agriculture export products such as sugar, coconuts, and bananas – having fallen away, national politicians could now deal with local bosses directly (Vartavarian 2019b). President Gloria Macapagal Arroyo even relied on one of Mindanao's most notorious warlord clans, the Ampatuans, to help "win" the 2004 election (marred by accusations of massive electoral fraud). It was only after the Ampatuans' 2009 massacre of members of a rival political clan and several accompanying journalists (with a total of fifty-eight killed) that forced Arroyo to distance herself from her warlord allies (Arguillas 2011).

Duterte's Neo-Bossism in Davao

In the late Marcos period, Davao was dubbed the murder capital of the Philippines.[6] Crony plunder, particularly of the banana industry controlled by the local bossist Floirendo family, "proved so destructive that Davao became a major area of NPA operations, with the most flagrant violence occurring in Davao City itself" (Vartavarian 2019b). The area became heavily militarized, as the AFP began targeting communist infiltration, which included organizing strikes and assassinations by NPA "sparrow units." Grisly killings by *Alsa Masa*, a vigilante group set up to fight communists in Davao, gained particular notoriety. Claiming to be "freedom fighters" trying to free the city from communist influence, they also benefited from NPA defections after a vicious purge in the local CPP branch in search of "Deep Penetration Agents" from the military (Abinales 1996). A hardline military commander in Davao, Lt. Col. Franco Calida, supported the vigilantes. By early 1987, the group was reported to have 3,000 members, many of them former communists, patrolling the streets on the lookout for leftist militants (May 1992, 18–22; also Collier 1995). With this confluence of the three major forms of political violence, "Davao City was awash with arms and highly trained triggermen" (Vartavarian 2019a). This provided the context in which Duterte developed a new paradigm of political violence.

Duterte's family had migrated to Davao from Danao City, Cebu where Duterte's father Vicente had served as mayor but who now followed his political patron, Alejandro Almendras, to Davao province which was then still considered a frontier zone. When the latter became a senator, Vicente served as governor of Davao from 1959 to 1966. Duterte's father was later appointed as Secretary of the Department of General Services during Marcos' legal presidency before making a 1967 run for Congress in a new Davao congressional district. He felt betrayed when Marcos and his *Nacionalista* Party refused to support his candidacy. Vicente died suddenly of a heart condition after his surprise electoral defeat (Parreño 2019, chp. 7). Duterte's father's bitter falling out with Marcos was later airbrushed out of the family history when Duterte successfully sought support from the Marcos family in his 2016 presidential

---

[6] Duterte was seen by his supporters to have drastically reduced crime in the "Wild West"-like southern city (Peel 2017). But the murder rate remained the country's highest when Duterte ran for president in 2016 as the Davao Death Squad was killing small-time, largely urban poor drug users and dealers, a pattern soon to be replicated at the national level.

campaign. In late 2021 Duterte's daughter, Sara, cemented this familial alliance by joining Marcos, Jr. as his vice presidential bet for the 2022 elections.

Duterte's mother, Soledad "Soling" Duterte, was a leading anti-Marcos oppositionist in Davao after the Aquino assassination in which regular rallies took place in imitation of the "confetti" revolution in the business district of Makati in Metro Manila (Reyes 2019). As mayor, Duterte was backed by businessman Jose "Chito" V. Ayala, a Cory Aquino loyalist, and also a close ally of her son Noynoy Aquino who later became president (Regalado 2021). Thanks to these strong "yellow" connections, Duterte was appointed Davao City vice mayor by Cory Aquino's administration and then won the race for mayor in 1988.

Duterte has often been misunderstood as a typical political boss who happened to be the first to win the presidency directly after holding local office. In reality, Duterte created a novel form of warlord violence which can be termed "neo-bossism" as mayor of Davao City. It involved alliance building around marginalized enemies rather than focusing on eliminating political rivals or intimidating the electorate.[7] Moving to curb violence in the city, Duterte struck a deal with the communists, offering them safe passage if they entered the city unarmed, and turning paramilitaries away from anti-communism toward the fight against crime. This was the beginning of a close relationship with the CPP, including its leader Jose Maria Sison who had been his former university professor, until their bitter breakup after failed peace talks as president, discussed in the next section.[8]

Duterte established the notorious Davao Death Squad (DDS) which employed policemen and ex-communist rebels to target purported drug criminals (Reyes 2016, 124). This allowed Duterte to triangulate between the communist rebels and the military while winning popular support by targeting supposed wrongdoers with vigilantes. He "concentrated organized violence into the hands of personal retainers and converted the Davao City Police into his own private army," making him the unchallenged urban warlord of the city who delivered "a basic, if harsh, stability" (Vartavarian 2019b). Vigilante killings continued, but now were largely the work of the DDS. A Davao-based rights

---

[7] An exception was the murder of the former spokesperson for *Alsa Masa* turned political opponent and journalist, Jun Pala, which according to a member of the DDS was ordered by Duterte after he became angered by the Pala's repeated attacks on the drug war and corruption accusations in his Davao radio show (*Philippine Daily Inquirer*, September 15, 2016; The *Philippine Star*, February 20, 2017).

[8] Duterte appears to have strongly influenced ideologically by Sison, which may explain why he called himself a "socialist" during the 2016 campaign and also stressed his nationalist credentials (Teehankee 2016). Scalice (2020) shows the CPP leadership tacitly supported Duterte in that election and condoned his drug war both in Davao and in the early years of his presidency. Also see Claudio and Abinales 2017.

group documented 1,424 killings by the DDS, a claim confirmed by a former DDS hit man turned whistleblower who submitted an affidavit to the International Criminal Court (ICC) (Reyes 2016, 114; Rappler Investigative Team 2021a and 2021b). Payments were provided for every person killed with bodies buried in mass graves or at sea. A 2009 human rights report (Human Rights Watch 2009) documented execution-style killings. Most victims were alleged drug dealers, petty criminals, or street children. A glossy 2002 piece in *Time* magazine dubbed Duterte "The Punisher" (a Marvel Comics vigilante anti-hero), noting his punitive streak as the "swaggering new-sheriff-in town" (Miller 2018, 171). The piece demonstrated Duterte's popular appeal to *Dabawenyos*, the city's citizens, which would soon capture the imagination of Filipinos nationally.

As long as political violence occurred outside of Metro Manila, it usually received limited attention in the national media while raising few questions about whether liberal democracy was being seriously eroded by such extreme coercion (Franco and Abinales 2007; Boudreau 2009; Reyes 2016). But Duterte's presidency brought his Davao-based version to national and global attention. What Sidel (2012) has termed the Philippines' long history of "subnational authoritarianism" had now been nationalized.

Nationalizing Neo-Bossism

In 2016, Duterte used his Davao drug war as his calling card to win the Philippine presidency (Teehankee and Thompson 2016). A Filipino sociologist (David 2016) influentially termed the "dark charisma" he exercised over voters "Dutertismo." Duterte promised to "restore order and respect for authority" by targeting "criminals, drug peddlers, and corrupt public officials." By articulating "the exasperation and desperation that the people experience in their daily lives," his campaign unleashed "a torrent of aggressive and resentful impulses not previously seen in our society, except perhaps in social media." Duterte repeatedly said during the campaign: "If you are not prepared to kill and be killed, you have no business being president of this country" (David 2016).

Duterte won the presidency with nearly 40 percent of the vote, a solid plurality in a five-way race with no run-off and in which there were no major accusations of vote fraud. Opinion poll survey data show the traction Duterte gained with this violent populist messaging, with the fight against illegal drugs going from a lower-level concern to the public's top priority in Pulse Asia surveys of January, February, and April 2016. Strikingly, just a few months after Duterte's election, poverty, jobs, inflation, and corruption again overtook criminality as the major concerns (see Figure 1).

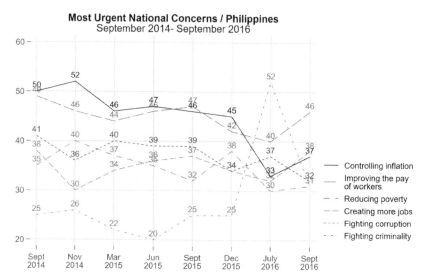

Figure 1 Most urgent national concerns/Philippines September 2014–
September 2016

Sources: Data from Pulse Asia. Ulat Ng Bayan, National Survey on Urgent National and
Local Concerns September 2014 www.pulseasia.ph/

Quimpo (2017) shows the successful securitization of the drugs issue
involved taking a major but containable problem in the Philippines,
according to the government's own statistics, and turning it into
a national emergency to be dealt with through any means necessary, no
matter how violent (see also Lasco 2016). Following the script he had used
when mayor of Davao, Duterte touted his crackdown as a public service
aimed at ridding cities of the scourge of drugs and to prevent the
Philippines from becoming a narco-state.

A survey by Maxwell (2019) has shown that while most Filipinos consider
drugs to be a minor to moderate problem in their own localities, influenced by
Duterte's political rhetoric which has been amplified by social media,
a majority believed drugs to be a serious national issue. This explains why
even after the election, when Filipinos became less concerned about how drug
dealing and abuse affected their own lives, they remained convinced that
violent "remedies" to "solve" the country's now securitized drug problem
were justified.

By employing a violent populist discourse, Duterte mobilized a mass con-
stituency through the media, particularly via social media and government-
sponsored trolling (Aim 2016; Cabañes and Cornelio 2017; Dreisbach 2018;
Ong and Cabañes 2018; Combinido 2019; Ong, Tapsell, and Curato 2019;
Combinido and Curato 2021). During his 2016 presidential campaign,

Duterte's messaging was ascendant on Facebook, the dominant social media platform in the Philippines, with 64 percent of election-related conversations taking place on his site (cited in Kho 2019, 4), although television still remained the most important source of information for voters in their choice of president (Holmes 2016). By the 2019 midterm election campaign, Duterte's allies had fully integrated digital disinformation into their campaigns (Ong, Tapsell, and Curato 2019). The "dark side of this trend" on social media was "the emergence of hyper-partisan platforms … that exploit citizens' mistrust against the political establishment" that was widely seen to have been represented by the opposition which in turn performed poorly in this election (Ong, Tapsell, and Curato 2019, 5).

A year earlier, in 2018, Facebook executive Katie Harbath had labeled the Philippines "patient zero" in disinformation on the social media platform. She elaborated that the election of Duterte as president of the Philippines backed by a massive and misleading online campaign proved to be the beginning of a global trend – "a month later it was Brexit, and then Trump got the nomination, and then the US elections" (cited in Combinido and Curato 2021, 19). Combinido (2019) argues the Philippines since Duterte's presidency has been similar to Vladimir Putin's Russia with his "troll army … paid to threaten citizens and bully journalists critical of Duterte." Celebrity pro-Duterte social media practitioners and bloggers were hired by the government to defend its actions and minimize human rights concerns (Dreisbach 2018). Such disinformation has "debased discourse and silenced dissidents in their vociferous sharing of fake news and amplification of hate speech" (Ong and Cabañes 2018, 1).

Creative industries in the Philippines proved vulnerable to pro-Duterte forces who have recruited "highly skilled, if corruptible, disinformation architects to collude with them without industry self-regulation mechanisms and sanctions in place." (Ong and Cabañes 2018, 1; also Ong and Cabañes 2019). It is "[i]ndustrial in its scope and organization, strategic in its outlook and expertise, and exploitative in its morality and ethics" (Ong and Cabañes 2018, 3).

The "War on Drugs"

As discussed in the Introduction, Duterte's rise to power parallels the ascendancy of other illiberal populist demagogues who have drawn on the "globalization of rage" given "massive disparities of wealth, power, education, and status" (Mishra 2016; see also Putzel 2020). But the drug war is the *differentia specifica*. Duterte has inscribed his politics on "the battered and bloodied bodies" of his victims (McCoy 2017, 5). A leading global expert on anti-drug campaigns (Collins 2016a) pointed out after a review of the global literature that "the failures of the 'war on drugs' have been well documented." He predicted from the outset that "the Philippines' new 'war' will fail and society will emerge worse off from it." He further warned against "widespread criminalization or any other 'pigheaded' antidrug policies" (Collins2016a, 2016b).

Duterte, of course, ignored such expert advice which in fact proved prescient. Besides the terrible toll of the killings as well large number of arrests which swelled the prison population, the violent campaign did not lead to a reduction in supply of illegal narcotics, as the country's top police drug official admitted in early 2020 (Allard and Lema 2020). Rather than deal with illegal drugs as a health problem, Duterte portrayed them as an all-encompassing menace to society in order to criminalize the issue and justify increased state repression (Regilme 2021a).

When Duterte launched his anti-drug *Blitzkrieg*, suspects died in "encounters" with police, were shot by motorcycle-riding gunmen, or were killed in raids by police "death squads" (Amnesty International 2019; Bello 2019). Their taped-up bodies were often displayed with a cardboard confessional sign strapped around their necks saying, "I am a pusher" or "drug lord" as well as "don't follow my example" and dumped on a road, under a bridge, or in a neighboring town. Reporters were brought to crime scenes and the police held regular press conferences in which they touted a growing body count as a sign of the success of the campaign. The guilt of victims was assumed, never proven, seriously investigated, or even questioned by authorities.

Duterte and his enforcers had lists of alleged drug users and dealers compiled at the local barangay level through a process known as *tokhang* – a portmanteau combining the Cebuano words *tuktok* (knock) and *hangyo* (plead). The 160,000 members of the Philippine National Police were ordered to ignore protocols concerning the use of deadly force (Lucero and Mangahas 2016). Internal reports as well as investigations by human rights groups show the police developed a template in which suspects were regularly reported to have "fought back" (*nanlaban*) with weapons planted next to the victims (Amnesty International 2019). This meant that "extrajudicial police vigilantism involving killings by on-duty police officers" were "masked as 'legitimate encounters' with criminals" (Kreuzer 2016). Most of those murdered were underprivileged young man in urban areas, suggesting poor Filipinos' lives mattered little (Thompson 2016). Many had surrendered to the authorities or were recently released prisoners, making it easier to portray the killings as targeting the "guilty" while denying them any form of due process. Employing counterinsurgency strategies to create penal borders, police would surround targeted barangays and effectively turn them into "killing zones" (Warburg and Jensen 2018).

During the initial, acclamatory phase, the drug war was highly performative, with violence a form of political messaging used to demonstrate to the growing ranks of the president's supporters that he was serious about ridding the country of the drug menace (Reyes 2016; Magcamit and Arugay 2017). But Duterte began adopting a more defensive strategy by early 2017. He accused domestic and foreign media as well as international organizations of exaggerating the numbers killed and propagating fake news. He also undertook an illiberal realignment of Philippine foreign policy away from the United States, and the West more generally, toward China which of course did not criticize his human rights record (Suorsa and Thompson 2018). The government also launched a disinformation campaign to offset criticism while obfuscating existing data about the numbers killed in the drug war (Philippine Center for Investigative Journalism 2017). Duterte unleashed invective-laden attacks on critics: human rights groups, the US government, and the European Union (Regilme 2021b). Duterte withdrew the Philippines from the ICC after it opened an investigation (the ICC, however, has continued its investigation of crimes committed during his presidency). He contrasted foreigners' human rights complaints with his strong popular support in the Philippines. Not a typical pro-US Filipino politician envisioned by the neo-colonial theory of Philippine politics (Quimpo 2008, 42–43), Duterte's "resurgent nationalism" allowed him to deflect international criticism of his drug war and demonstrate political will while making his domestic opponents appear traitorous (Teehankee 2016).

Duterte's Militarized COVID-19 Response

In response to the COVID-19 pandemic, populist strongmen like Brazil's Jair Bolsonaro and the US's Donald Trump practiced "medical populism" – ignoring scientific advice, proffering denials, and blaming others (Lasco 2020b). More technocratic leaders recognized the severity of the pandemic, implementing strict lockdowns. But some failed to adopt more flexible restrictions once testing improved due to local enforcement difficulties, which can be termed "blunt force regulation" (van der Kamp 2021). Although neither a pandemic denialist nor an obtuse technocrat, Duterte's response combined aspects of both approaches, with blame shifting and one-size-fits-all lockdowns while also securitizing the crisis.

Despite also engaging in a "masculinity contest" like many other illiberal populist leaders, Duterte quickly "shapeshifted" from claiming invincibility to the face of the pandemic to acting as the nation's strongman protector against it (Parmanand 2020). Utilizing methods developed during his war on drugs, Duterte imposed a heavily militarized approach, scapegoated supposedly disobedient Filipinos (*pasaway*), and bullied local politicians. The Philippines was one of the worst pandemic performers globally, ranked at the bottom of Bloomberg's global pandemic "resilience" index of fifty-three countries (Bloomberg 2021; see also Sarao 2021), based on vaccination coverage, virus containment, the severity of lockdowns, quality of health care, progress toward restarting travel, and the overall mortality throughout the pandemic. Yet Duterte's approval ratings remained robust, with his "brute force governance" undermining the dynamics of accountability, enabling him to win public approval despite policy failure (Thompson 2022b).

In early April 2020, Duterte denounced protestors demonstrating against lockdown restrictions because of growing hunger and notoriously ordered the police to "shoot them dead." Aggressive lockdown enforcement resulted "in multiple incidents of abuse by police and deputized civilian officials" (Talabong 2020). This was not surprising as police were using "the same rules of engagement in the pandemic" as they had during the anti-drug campaign (Gavilan and Talabong 2020).

It soon became evident that Duterte had found a scapegoat to justify these indiscriminate but largely ineffective lockdown measures given a lack of testing and tracing. He blamed the *pasaway* – hardheaded, irresponsible Filipinos – for supposedly not obeying pandemic regulations as responsible for the continued spread of the disease (Lasco 2020a; Hapal 2021). Elaborating on the significance of this blame game, Hapal (2021, 10–11) suggests by "arresting the *pasaway*, the government is, in effect, protecting the well-being of law-abiding Filipino citizens" which reinforces a "war-like narrative," justifying "intense policing." Filipinos' supposed lack of discipline created a need for a stern authority figure, "*Tatay* (Daddy) Digong," as the Philippine president is popularly known by his supporters. But this was pure scapegoating as surveys show they were among the most obedient citizens globally in following quarantine regulations (Punongbayan 2020).

Besides singling out the *pasaway* for blame, Duterte also bullied local governments into submission, with national police and military taking over key roles during the pandemic. Duterte had already centralized national power over local governments earlier in his presidency despite a (broken) promise to make constitutional changes to turn the country into a federal system (Gera and Hutchcroft 2021).[9] But Duterte's centralization of power disguised the national government's "weak steering" which therefore was more reliant on "strong-arming" local

---

[9] Although Duterte had set up a Constitutional Committee to map out charter change, he soon lost interest in the topic (Teehankee 2019). The irony is that Duterte, although a provincial outsider who often railed against "Imperial Manila," has done more to tighten the grip of the Manila-centric Philippine state over local politicians since martial law under Marcos (Hutchcroft and Gera 2022).

officials to implement policies than on regularized bureaucratic regulations (Hutchcroft and Gera 2022). The dysfunctional relationship between the national and local governments became particularly apparent during delays in vaccine procurement in 2021 in which it was the slowest country in Southeast Asia to receive the vaccines and to ramp up inoculations.

A militarized approach, the scapegoating of the urban poor, and the bullying of local politicians was a strategy Duterte had already fashioned during his drug war. The foundering of his COVID-19 strategy paralleled the failure of the drug war to reduce the supply of drugs. But it too shifted blame toward a securitized enemy, the small-time drug addict/dealer in the former, the *pasaway* in the latter.

Conclusion

Rebellion, counterinsurgency, and warlordism have long plagued local politics in the Philippines. All three forms of political violence worsened during the Marcos period, with the southern city of Davao becoming an epicenter. It was there Duterte forged his violent populist messaging with warlord-style coercion, albeit with a twist. He reversed the logic of local political bossism while retaining its violent tactics by targeting supposed urban poor criminals more than his political rivals in an anti-insurgency-style anti-drugs campaign which wooed rather than intimidated voters. A political innovator, Duterte built upon but also transformed traditions of local political violence in the Philippines which he implemented as president. Political violence which had once been localized as "sub-national authoritarian" was now fully nationalized. Duterte also employed his strategy of securitizing problems and scapegoating the urban poor in other policy areas, particularly in his highly militarized but ineffective response to the pandemic.

Duterte was not the first Philippine president to make extensive use of political violence to aggrandize power. Quirino had relied upon local warlords to intimidate opposition in his presidential election campaign in 1949. As a young man Marcos, Sr., was convicted of killing his father's chief political rival (Gomez 2015). In his controversial reelection campaign in 1969, Marcos employed not just local paramilitaries but also national military force, which he had increasingly brought under his personal control in the run-up to declaring martial law in 1972 (Berlin 1982; Brillantes 1987, 37–47; Kessler 1989).

4 Deflecting from Mass Poverty

In Section 2 it was argued that the Philippines' recent democratic backsliding is due to Duterte's transgression of democratic norms in a weakly institutionalized patronage-driven democracy like Quezon and Marcos had before him. In Section 3 it was shown how Duterte relied heavily on political violence as

Quirino and Marcos also had. A further key element receives closer examination in this section: the politics of decrying but also deflecting from the persistence of mass poverty.

For over a century – from the US colonial period, during early independence, the martial law era, and since the people power uprising – social reforms have been promised to "uplift the whole Filipino people." But instead of implementing redistributive land reform and other effective development strategies that would actually have improved the well-being of the worst off, state policies have been largely ineffectual in lessening high levels of inequality and aiding the poorest in society. As regime types have shifted from *de facto* one-party rule during the Commonwealth to a competitive two-party system after independence, authoritarian rule under Marcos, and multi-partyism after the fall of the dictatorship, the lack of pro-poor reforms have been used during all these different forms of government as a justification for political change. Pseudo-reform programs were then employed to divert attention away from the persistence of mass poverty. Most recently, Duterte's drug war has been largely a "war against the poor," with urban poor petty drug users and dealers targeted while mass poverty persisted (Thompson 2016). But it proved effective in legitimizing his highly illiberal rule.

Colonial Democracy and the First Failed Land Reform

The transition to export-oriented commercial agriculture during the late Spanish colonial period was rapid and largely successful in market terms, although at the price of creating an increasingly impoverished class of peasant tenants. With population nearly tripling in the nineteenth century (to 6.5 million by 1898), family land plots were subdivided and became increasingly uneconomical. The landholdings of the religious orders, the friar estates, expanded, often through land grabbing. The renting out of small parcels of land to peasants created the *kasama* or share-tenancy system. Through these means, an "evolving colonial elite" accumulated the "best land for export crops and a labor force" to cultivate it (Amoroso and Abinales 2017, 81-82). Peasant grievances helped spark the revolution against Spain in the late nineteenth century (Borras 2007, 83–84).

Under US colonial rule, the Philippines had a dependent, commodity export-oriented economy with a powerful landed class but also growing social unrest, as discussed in the previous section. US officials prioritized coopting local elites who won elections, with suffrage initially limited to the landed, in a "colonial democracy." This created a patronage-based system which furthered wealth concentration (Paredes 1989). By bringing together in Manila provincial, largely agrarian elites elected to the Philippine Assembly established in 1907, the United States created a national ruling class self-conscious of its political and economic power (Anderson 1988).

In 1903, William Howard Taft, the first American governor-general of the Philippines (and future US president and supreme court chief justice), ordered the sale of the Spanish Catholic friar estates to their peasant cultivators. This was part of the US effort to emphasize the enlightened character of their colonial project, contrasting it with the "Dark Age of Spanish rule ... despotic, tyrannical, medieval" (Garcia 2005). The redistribution of the religious orders' estates was also intended to mitigate what was (rightly) seen as a potential source of peasant grievance. But while farmers on village plots within the friar estates did receive land, the other half of the estates consisting of yet unfarmed land was sold to American business interests and Filipino elites. Moreover, this partial "land reform" did not provide the support necessary to make land transfer a success for the new peasant cultivators, who lacked access to credit and farm equipment. Not surprisingly, many of the new freeholders lapsed into debt, so that most of their recently acquired lands ended up in the hands of landed elites even as the poor often stayed on as tenants (Amoroso and Abinales 2017, 122). It was the first of series of failed land reforms.

Despite decrying the injustices of Spanish colonialism and promising social reform, in practice US colonial officials showed little interest in "uplifting 'the whole Filipino people'," as they had promised as part of their justification for conquering the Philippines (Luton 1971, 70–71, cited in Amoroso and Abinales 2017, 123). On the contrary, during the American colonial period, landlessness increased steadily (Borras 2007, 84). This failure to bring about social change "condemned the vast majority of Filipinos" to "crushing" inequality, perpetuating rigid social hierarchies and encouraging predatory elite behavior (Abinales and Amoroso 2017, 157).[10] The precedent of pledging to help the poorest Filipinos in order to deflect from a concentration of power in a "democratic" political system had been set.

Quezon's Pseudo-Social Justice Policy

During the Commonwealth period, President Manuel Quezon promised major social reforms to preempt the demands of the Sakdals and the Partido Komunista ng Pilipinas (PKP), discussed in the previous section. The huge

---

[10] Another significant initiative during the early American colonial period also had adverse consequences for the poor – the Torrens land titling system. Meant to codify private land ownership to aid economic development, it overrode informal understandings of land use by indigenous communities. In practice, it enabled land grabbing by elites who understood the law and had access to courts while displacing poor peasants who did not understand the new system and had no access to the land survey registration system (Borras 2007, 84).

Sakdalista rebellion of 1935 had demonstrated the degree of peasant discontent and alarmed the government (Sturtevant 1976, 241). Made up largely of landless peasants, the Sakdals had demanded reduced taxation of the poor and radical land reform based on the redistribution of elite-owned estates as part of a revolutionary uprising against US colonial rule seen to have maintained an unjust social order (Terami-Wada 1988). PKP organizational successes during the same period revealed similar discontent among lowly paid manual workers.

Quezon pledged to enact "legislation which would solve once and for all the problem of the relationship between the tenants and the landowners especially in the large estates," warning "history is replete with instances when in their wrath the people have revolted and by force deprived the landlords of their possessions" (cited in Arcellana 1961). Accordingly, Quezon's "social justice" policy proposals in 1939 included a plan to break up large landholdings and distribute them to cultivators, create a resettlement program for the landless in frontier areas, mandate a minimum wage and an eight-hour working day, guarantee the right to form peasant groups and labor unions, and increase access to courts to settle disputes with factory owners and landholders. But promises of major social change also conveniently deflected from an ideological vacuum created by the creation of the Commonwealth (Amoroso and Abinales 2017, 149). Quezon's promise "to lift the 'yoke of oppression' long borne by the Filipino masses" was but a "transparent attempt to recapture and ideological consensus lost with the granting of independence" (McCoy 1989, 139).

While some of Quezon's proposed measures were passed, including the minimum wage and limited working hours, intense opposition by large estate owners led Quezon to abandon his land reform proposals, instead increasing land resettlement in Mindanao (Abinales and Amoroso 2017, 154). Quezon later even lent his support to landlord legislators' efforts to repeal the moderate Rice Share Tenancy Act of 1933, although after intense public pressure he ultimately vetoed it. Disillusioned by Quezon's abandonment of much of this program, socialist leader Pedro Abad Santos bitterly remarked the poor "can expect nothing from President Quezon because he is also a landlord . . . His so-called social-justice is a farce" (McCoy 1989, 139).

Magsaysay and Macapagal: Land Reform Falls Short Again

Two presidents during the early independence, pre-martial period (1946–72), Ramon Magsaysay and Disodado P. Macapagal, emphasized the necessity of agrarian reform. As discussed in Section 2, Ramon Magsaysay had defeated incumbent President Quirino in the 1953 presidential election. Promising to end corruption, he cultivated a "man of the people" image and promised land to the tillers – although the *Nacionalista* Party platform he ran on actually downplayed the issue as its leaders were opposed to major agrarian change. With surveys showing most voters had little understanding of the details of his land reform proposal, Magsaysay won substantial electoral support from the poor peasantry without alienating wealthy landowners (Starner 1961, 97–99). From the American colonial period to early independence, tenancy had increased dramatically, reaching nearly 90 percent in Central Luzon by the late 1940s where the Huk insurgency was concentrated, with absentee land ownership common (King 1977, 319). According to one sympathetic scholar (Wurfel 1958), Magysaysay was "intensely concerned with the improvement of tenant-landlord relations" and felt impelled to end the injustice of "landlord oppression."

As president, Magsaysay launched a direct outreach program to rural communities through a new executive office he created that delivered government assistance to farmers, with the US government providing funding and nongovernment organizations, most notably the Philippine Rural Reconstruction Movement, aiding these efforts (Abinales and Amoroso 2017, 179–182). In 1955, Magsaysay introduced bills to Congress to regulate tenancy and redistribute large estates to their peasant tillers. But congressional landlord opposition weakened the legislation considerably by imposing a large landholding retention limit (Riedinger 1995, 88). More successful were efforts, as had been the case under Quezon, to resettle landless families in frontier areas of Mindanao. But this exacerbated tensions between Christian settlers and Muslims in Mindanao, with the latter's ancestral domains often encroached upon, leading to a sense of Moro marginalization in their own lands (Tuminez 2007). The United States, which had strongly backed Magsaysay's presidential campaign, seemed to lose interest in social reform in the Philippines after the Huk rebellion declined by the mid-1950s, refusing to lobby on land issues and even recalling American advisers who had called for far-reaching agrarian redistribution (Abinales and Amoroso 2017, 179–182). The conservative land program during the Magsaysay administration was not "redistributionist" as was agrarian reform undertaken about the same time in Taiwan in which absentee land ownership had been abolished and a low ceiling imposed on land retention to the benefit of the landless (Putzel 1992, 73–74).

Less than a decade later, Macapagal, a self-proclaimed "poor boy from Lubao" (his birth city in the province in Pampanga) became president. During the 1961 election, he portrayed the incumbent, Carlos P. Garcia, as corrupt and out of touch with the common man. Yet similar to Magsaysay, Macapagal was in fact a member of the provincial elite rather than a man from the masses. Concerned about the revival of communist insurgency based on agrarian grievances given the rise of communism elsewhere in Southeast Asia, Macapagal lobbied Congress to enact the Agricultural Land Reform Code in 1963. But again, like Magsaysay's, Quezon's, and Taft's failed land redistribution initiatives, it proved of little help to poor tenant farmers. The law provided for the abolition of tenancy, imposed limitations on land ownership, and established a Land Bank to purchase, divide, and then resell large estates to small farmers (Takigawa 1964, 74–76). But a still landlord-dominated Congress imposed high land retention limits and allowed for the exclusion of large estates classified as being of economic importance. Landlords could "eject" tenants, but actually then keep them on as wage laborers (Boyce 1993, 135). Moreover, the program was woefully underfunded. The economic condition of most Filipino farmers actually worsened during this time, with the average peasant tilling less land and becoming more debt ridden than before Macapagal's "land reform" had been implemented (Hayami, Quisumbing, and Andriano 1990).

Marcos' Failed Developmentalist Authoritarianism

If Quezon, Magsaysay, and Macapagal had promised social reform to bolster political campaigns and elicit broader-based support for their presidencies, Marcos went one step further by using land redistribution as a major justification for the declaration of martial law in 1972. He "dexterously" manipulated public opinion with the "rhetoric of social reform" to build up "a broad base of support for his 'New Society'" (Paredes 1989, 1). "Despite strong misgivings about the authoritarian character of Marcos' regime, many Filipinos shared his critique of the 'old society'," with anger directed by state propaganda toward the "reactionary oligarchs" controlling Congress (Paredes 1989, 1).

Marcos' Presidential Decree No. 27 in 1972 promised to redistribute all tenanted rice and corn lands. Land was to be purchased below market value and its sale subsidized to landless beneficiaries with long payment periods and with land retention limits substantially lowered from the high levels set under Macapagal. Resettlement efforts for the landless were also accelerated (Borras 2007, 86).

Yet the results of Marcos' "Operation Land Transfer" fell far below the high expectations raised. Led by the newly created Department of Agrarian Reform (DAR), the government claimed nearly a half a million small farmers received land while nearly 700,000 received leasehold contracts awarded to tenants (Putzel 1992, 138–139; Abinales and Amoroso 2017, 209). This meant that less the one sixth of land under rice and corn cultivation was redistributed (Boyce 1993, 136). Furthermore, because the program was limited to rice and corn (but with landlords allowed to switch farm land usage), other key commercial crops, particularly coconut, sugar, and banana growing areas were excluded, which were conveniently dominated by Marcos cronies. Questions have also been raised about whether supposed peasant beneficiaries were actually able to pay for the land and ultimately received titles to it (Borras 2007, 87). Landlords pressured tenants in various ways: denying them access to irrigation, filing civil and criminal cases no matter how specious, evicting them from housing, and threatening outright physical violence (Fegan 1979, 243–244, 323–329, cited in Boyce 1993, 135). In addition, indigenous communities with traditional understandings of land use were excluded and subject to land grabbing. Like in Macapagal's reform, farm laborers were ineligible for redistribution, in principle because wage labor was socially acceptable while tenancy was not, but in practice due to political expediency (Boyce 1993, 135).

The reform program was, as similar initiatives had been in the past, riddled with loopholes. It is thus not surprising that despite the fanfare surrounding the initiative – Marcos termed it "the only gauge for the success or failure of the New Society" – DAR and peasant groups estimates show nearly 70 percent of the total agricultural population remained landless or near landless a little more than a decade and a half after the program began (Boyce 1993, 135.; Borras 2007, 88). Even this may be an underestimate of the continued scope of land hunger as landlords feared divulging the status of tenants on their property could lead them to be subject to the redistributive measures (Borras 2007, 88). While some large rice haciendas were broken up and some well-connected tenants did benefit from the program, it utterly failed to aid "the poorest and possibly most numerous stratum of Philippine rural society, the landless," and likely even "worsened their plight" (Boyce 1993, 136–137).

Marcos had also promised a state-led industrial development program. Williamson and de Dios (2014) trace more than a half-century of industrialization in the Philippines before Marcos to the early twentieth century during the early American colonial period with the rise of small-scale, labor-intensive manufacturing specialized in commodity processing. Continuing its industrial growth in the interwar period, Philippine industry underwent rapid expansion during post-war import substitution industrialization (ISI). Although ISI involved targeted government intervention in the form of tariff policies, it was not yet a systematic effort to create a "developmental state" with a variety of policy instruments – such as a development planning agency, the National Economic Development Agency, export processing zones, and industrial policy – created by Marcos. While new to the Philippines, these were instruments typical of developmental states in East Asia at the time (Haggard 2018). The Philippines has largely been excluded from this developmentalist literature because of its later economic failures. But Kang (2002) points to striking similarities between Marcos and South Korean dictator Park Chung-hee at the outset of their authoritarian rule.

Industrial exports rose significantly during early martial law as foreign investment increased, a massive infrastructure drive was launched, and plans were drawn up for eleven major industrial projects designed to push the country toward industrialization and make it the next Asian "tiger" economy. But to pay for these ambitious undertakings, Marcos borrowed freely from international markets awash in petrodollars after oil price increases in 1973. The Philippines' foreign debt nearly quintupled from 1974 to 1980 to over $17 billion and reached over $26 billion by 1985 (Dohner and Intal 1989, 392). These debt levels, greenlighted by the International Monetary Fund with which Marcos long enjoyed good relations, proved unsustainable when crisis hit (Slayton and Thompson 1985).

The Philippine economy, already slowing by the late 1970s, nosedived after the Aquino assassination in 1983. Revelations that the Central Bank had falsified the country's financial records (much like Greece would be caught doing twenty-five years later) led to capital flight, the Philippine peso to plummet, inflation to skyrocket, and the government to ask for a debt moratorium. The crisis ejected the Philippines from "the industrial catch-up club" to which it has never returned (Williamson and de Dios 2014, 50). Gross domestic product (GDP) fell 10 percent, with per capita income falling even faster (Boyce 1993, 39). It took two decades before pre-crisis income levels were regained (Bautista 2003). By the end of Marcos' rule, two-thirds of families were experiencing at least mild hunger and 22 percent of preschool children were found to be seriously malnourished (Boyce 1993, 47–50). The "New Society" had turned out to be worse than the old.

Marcos was not an "authoritarian developmentalist" leader of the same caliber as South Korea's Park. A lawyer-politician, not a soldier-nationalist, Marcos did not distance himself from his loyalists, favoring cronies over technocrats (Hutchcroft 2011). Instead of using performance criteria to ensure export competitiveness despite close business-state ties as Park had insisted upon when giving state subsidies to giant conglomerates (*chaebols*) in South Korea, Marcos apportioned large sectors of the economy to his family and close friends, as discussed in Section 2. This centralized a long tradition of "booty capitalism" in the Philippines (Hutchcroft 1998). Thus, while Park's leadership led to "rapid industrialization in Korea," Marcos' rule resulted in "disastrous economic predation in the Philippines" (Hutchcroft 2011, 542).

Growth but Little Poverty Reduction after People Power

The post-people power order was premised on democratizing the country after a decade and a half of dictatorship, stabilizing an economy in crisis, and undertaking social reforms promised but never effectively implemented during martial rule. Cory Aquino and her favored successor who (narrowly) won a six-year presidency through 1998, Fidel Ramos, began a transition to democracy. A liberal constitution was promulgated in 1987, competitive legislative elections were held that same year, and steps were taken to improve human rights. They also achieved financial stability, restarted economic growth, and undertook efforts to recover Marcos' "hidden wealth" by the newly created Philippine Commission on Good Government. But as had often been the case in the past, social reform proved to be the Achilles heel, with little poverty reduction, limited success with land reform as well as continued substandard health care and education during their presidencies.

Poverty fell by 10 percent from 1985 to 2000. But there was rapid population growth as the Aquino government – "pliant to the wishes" of the Catholic Church – dismantled Marcos-era birth control policies (Lasco 2017). Thus, the absolute numbers of impoverished Filipinos actually increased (Lasco 2017; Asian Development Bank 2005). Despite relatively high growth rates beginning in the early 1990s, government statistics (with a low poverty threshold) showed that even before the impact of the Asian Financial Crisis was felt in 1998, nearly two in five Filipinos were poor (Philippine Statistics Authority 2002). Using self-reporting, a Social Weather Stations survey found that a much larger number of Filipinos, nearly 60 percent, considered themselves impoverished at that time (Social Weather Stations 2021). Despite efforts to improve educational outcomes, two million school-age children had not acquired any formal schooling by the midpoint of Ramos' administration, with fewer than 40 percent of young people attending high school. Only about one-fourth of those who reported having been taken ill in a survey at the end of the first Aquino administration had access to health care. Nearly 90 percent of poor, pregnant women continued to deliver their babies at home. More than a third of the population did not have access to fresh drinking water (Raquiza 1997). "Relative to the goals set," the government's performance in poverty reduction during this period was disappointing (Bautista 2003).

Furthermore, the skewing of poverty in rural areas was striking. Rural incomes were about half of the average urban ones, with fewer government services available. In 1988, nearly 60 percent of the population lived in rural areas, three-fourths of them in agricultural households, and more than two-thirds of which were landless (Borras 2007, 87–88). In addition, due to a lack of irrigation, neglect of roads-to-market infrastructure, and massive deforestation, conditions in agricultural areas suffered from general decline (Bautista 2003). Life in the rural Philippines was "marked by poverty, uncertainty, hardship, and often violence," with the majority of peasants farming "small parcels of land" without adequate infrastructure or irrigation while millions had no access to land at all (Timberman 1991, 342).

Given massive poverty in rural areas, Cory Aquino, like previous presidents from Quezon to Marcos, unveiled an agrarian reform program, the Comprehensive Agrarian Land Reform Program (CARP). After initial hesitation – no surprise given that Aquino herself came from a family that owned one of the country's largest plantations, Hacienda Luisita – her administration acted after thirteen peasant protestors had been shot dead during a large demonstration demanding land reform held in front of the presidential palace, Malacañang, in January 1987. Once again a landlord-dominated Congress resisted. But the legislation was championed by outspoken progressive legislators backed by NGOs and peasant groups (Borras 2007, 106). Not surprisingly, landed interests gained the upper hand, leading to a relatively modest bill which, while not blatantly reactionary, was also not substantially redistributionist (Hayami, Quisumbing, and Andriano 1990; Putzel 1992; Riedinger 1995; Borras 2007, chp. 2).

As in previous efforts, CARP was plagued by high land purchase costs and inadequate funding. The land retention limit remained high and was relatively easy to circumvent. In addition, agricultural export sectors, like sugar, coconut, and bananas, were excluded from CARP for the first ten years of the program. Once again, national political elites were "reluctant to antagonize the land-owning classes with expropriationary land reform, but especially those engaged in agricultural exports" (Borras 2007, 100).

While the modest results of land reform are one reason for the persistence of poverty in the initial two administrations after people power, the decision to honor the country's enormous Marcos-era debt of USD twenty-eight billion was another. Despite some members of Cory Aquino's cabinet (notably Socio-Economic Planning Secretary and NEDA director Solita Monsod) advocating "selective repudiation" considering that it was largely the result of Marcos' kleptocracy, they were overruled by more conservative cabinet members insisting upon a negotiated restructuring with foreign creditors (Timberman 1991, 336). The Philippines, like many other developing countries, found itself caught in a "debt trap" in which it became a net exporter of capital. During Aquino's term, the government had to spend the equivalent of 10 percent of GDP to finance it. With debt payments consuming nearly half of the government's budget, this created a "vicious cycle" of higher interest rates and larger budget deficits (de Dios and Hutchcroft 2003, 53). This limited the government's ability to introduce welfare programs, build adequate infrastructure, or deal comprehensively with natural catastrophes (such as the 1990 volcanic eruption of Mount Pinatubo) (Abinales and Amoroso 2017, 243).

A third, more general reason is the discrediting of developmentalist strategies due to the corruption and cronyism of the Marcos regime (Ramos 2021). State-led industrial policy had been key to employment generation and poverty reduction elsewhere in the region but was assiduously avoided by Aquino's pro-market technocrats and subsequent post-Marcos presidents who largely adopted neoliberal policy prescriptions (M. Raquiza 2018).

The Ramos administration's ambitious economic plans succeeded in jump-starting the economy, attracting greater foreign investment, and improving infrastructure (the problem of regular electricity brownouts was largely resolved). The Philippines was able to weather the Asian Financial Crisis of 1997–98 better than most of its Southeast Asian neighbors, although this was also due to smaller financial bubbles in a slower-growing economy. In keeping with a "growth with equity strategy," Ramos launched the Social Reform Agenda (SRA) in 1994. But the government allocated less than a fifth of its budget to welfare projects, with most of this coming from foreign development assistance (Amoroso and Abinales 2017, 249). Ultimately, the SRA went "against the grain" of Ramos' otherwise neoliberal, market-oriented reforms, with "the contradictions between government word and action" becoming increasingly evident (Raquiza 1997).

Proletarian Populism and "No Corruption, No Poverty"

Given limited social reform and continued high poverty levels, there was a political role waiting to be filled by a politician making more credible promises to help the poor. Joseph E. Estrada played this part perfectly. He was a former movie star whose "proletarian potboilers" portrayed him as a lonely fighter for the disadvantaged against upper-class villains (Hedman 2001, 27). Elected senator in 1987 and vice president (separately elected in the Philippines) in 1992, he easily won the presidency in 1998, transforming his fans into his voters. Nicknamed "Erap," an inversion of "*pare*," (a Filipino slang for friend), he befriended the friendless poor. As president, he successfully guided the country through the fallout of the Asian financial crisis and made greater efforts than is commonly acknowledged to help disadvantaged Filipinos (Thompson 2014a). Estrada's record on social reform, like nearly everything during his presidency, is highly contested (for a critical view see Balisacan 2001). But considering he was only in power for thirty months before being overthrown, his creation of the National Anti-Poverty Commission and efforts to rejuvenate land reform (putting in place a motivated and technically adept team led by the highly regarded activist Horacio "Boy" Morales as Secretary of Agrarian reform) are worthy of note (Borras 2007, 249–251).

But Estrada soon faced charges of immorality (he was a self-confessed womanizer and gambler with a notorious "midnight cabinet") and corruption (of which Estrada was likely guilty but which did not differentiate him significantly from his predecessors or successors). He was impeached by the lower house but not convicted after a tumultuous senate trial. But Estrada was forced to step down after large protests. The insurrection was dubbed "EDSA Dos" as it also took place on Epifanio de los Santos Avenue where the uprising against President Ferdinand Marcos, also known as people power, had occurred (Landé 2001). Middle-class protestors were again backed by the "hegemonic bloc" of the Catholic Church hierarchy, big business leaders, civil society activists (with university students at the forefront), and, ultimately, the top military brass (Hedman 2001, 2006). Estrada may have discredited himself in the eyes of elites and the middle classes with his crude manners and corrupt ways, but his lower-class supporters rallied in a mass demonstration known as "EDSA Tres" or "Poor People's People Power" which nearly overthrew the successor government after Estrada was arrested on graft charges in April 2001.

Estrada was succeeded in office by Vice President Gloria Macapagal-Arroyo who had been elected in 1998 largely on the basis of her image as a reformer. But her legitimacy was weakened by taking power in an extra-constitutional manner and accusations she stole the 2004 presidential election from Estrada's friend and even more famous movie star Fernando Poe, Jr. (known as the Filipino John Wayne) who also ran on a proletarian populist platform. The "Hello Garci" scandal of 2005 revealed that Arroyo had been directly involved in the manipulation of the presidential election a year earlier (Hutchcroft 2008, 145–146). As part of her effort to regain popular support, Arroyo unveiled a major social policy initiative in 2007–08, the *Pantawid Pamilyang Pilipino* Program (Bridging Program for the Filipino Family Program), a conditional cash transfer (CCT) scheme aimed at eradicating extreme poverty through investments in the health and education of children via conditional assistance to their mothers. Encouraged by international financial institutions to combat the adverse impact of neoliberal policies in the 1990s and loosely modeled on Brazil's Bolsa Familia (Family Allowance program), CCT's rationale was to address "the intergenerational cycle of poverty, especially by developing human capital" (M. Raquiza 2018, 273–274). When a decade later it was shown CCT had no statistically significant impact in the Philippines, its defenders claimed its effect would only be felt in the long term as it "was not designed to be a quick fix to reduce poverty" (Albert, Dumagan, and Martinez 2015, 42, cited in M. Raquiza 2018, 274). At the same time, Arroyo placed all other "social-reform initiatives, including land reform . . . on the backburner" (Bello 2009, 4).

The Philippines enjoyed impressive macroeconomic growth averaging near or above 6 percent annually during Arroyo's presidency and that of her successor, Noynoy Aquino. But this was largely the result of service sector expansion and real estate speculation, not a revival of manufacturing which generates more employment (A. Raquiza 2018). Economic growth remained profoundly unequal, with the growth in the aggregate wealth of the country's forty richest families in 2011 equivalent to over three-quarters of the increase in the country's GDP in that year (Habito 2013). Noynoy Aquino increased mandatory schooling from ten to twelve years and successfully lobbied Congress to pass reproductive health legislation providing greater birth control access despite the vehement opposition of the Catholic Church hierarchy (with the conservative supreme court then overruling part of the legislation) (Takagi 2017; Dañguilan 2018). He also promised to complete the land reform initiative started during his mother's presidency three decades earlier (and which finally led to the redistribution of the Aquino–Cojuango family Hacienda Luisita in 2013).[11] CCT remained Aquino's "flagship anti-poverty program of choice even if it has yet to prove its effectiveness in the fight against poverty" given the weakness of flanking universal social welfare measures (M. Raquiza 2018, 282). The increase in CCT funding may also have been motivated by the desire of Aquino's Liberal Party for more patronage resources useful for elections which would have been better spent on providing more social services and boosting industrial policy to create more jobs (M. Raquiza 2018, 281–282). Although the official poverty rate dipped slightly, a quarter of the population was still forced to live on a dollar a day or less. Self-reported poverty remained high during his presidency, with about 50 percent of Filipinos describing themselves to pollsters as poor. This was an improvement over the over 70 percent during the severe economic crisis of the late Marcos era and the 60 percent under the first Aquino and Ramos administrations but had hardly changed despite over a decade and a half of solid growth since 2001 (Social Weather Stations 2021). Given the failure to substantially reduce poverty after people power and the subversion of a proletarian populist alternative, Rodrigo Duterte could plausibly claim he was ordinary Filipinos' "*ang huling baraha*," their "last card."

Political Legitimacy Despite a War Against the Poor

Like Marcos, Duterte blamed "the oligarchy" for the Philippines' developmental failures and used this to help justify his turn to overtly illiberal rule. But his "anti-oligarchy bark [was] worse than his bite" (Mendoza 2018, 78).

---

[11] Noynoy Aquino had promised to complete land reform but much land remained unredistributed by the end of his term. Although Hacienda Luisita was finally allotted to the plantation workers, peasant activists claimed the scheme to be a fraud, with Aquino's family allegedly using a phony lottery scheme to regain covert control over much of the property (Tupaz 2015).

Like previous presidents, Duterte was not hostile to the oligarchy per se but rather used this rhetoric to attack political enemies and favor his own cronies. Yet his predecessor's broken pledge to eliminate corruption and thus poverty had set the stage for simplistic solutions to the country's complex social problems, Duterte's "dystopian narrative" of the drug war. But this "comes at a price," Duterte warned, "the price of liberal rights" (Curato 2017, 7).

Another 2016 presidential candidate, then vice president, Jejomar "Jojo" Binay, campaigned on the pledge to expand nationally the social net he had created to aid poor residents in the business district of Metro Manila, Makati, significantly lowering poverty. Like Estrada and Poe, Binay appealed to poor Filipinos who had gained little from recent rapid economic growth, the benefits of which were largely confined to the rich and middle class (Keenan 2013). But his messaging was overshadowed by a selective senate investigation by Aquino allies into a scandal during his time as mayor. The undermining of the "good governance" narrative might not have led to a violent, illiberal populist turn had proletarian-style appeals not been consistently sidelined.

The popularity of the drug war across class lines suggested Duterte had successfully diverted the grievances of the poor away from the failures of social reform. Support for the drug war was high despite the fact that opinion polls showed 73 percent were worried (41 percent were "very worried") that they, or someone they knew, could become a victim of extrajudicial killing (Johnson and Fernquest 2018, 367). Anthropologists have investigated the views of the poor about the drug war. Kusaka (2017, 49; see also Jensen and Hapal 2018; Arguelles 2019) reported that his informants in an urban poor neighborhood "largely accept" that the drug war aims to create a "moral citizenry" while excluding those who do not adhere to civic values and thus become "undeserving of rescue." It was believed that "good citizens" would be saved while victims were "immoral others."

Duterte's highly militarized approach to the COVID-19 pandemic also proved popular. As discussed in Section 3, *pasaway*, the ill-disciplined, were also imagined to be primarily urban poor males, the main target of the drug war. Amplified by Duterte's illiberalism, this construct brought together "a range of different negative traits with implicit class contempt," legitimizing a heavy-handed response to control the *Lumpenproletariat* (Hapal 2021, 10–11). Long, inflexible lockdowns did little to reduce the spread of the virus because in "a developing country like the Philippines, where a large number of the urban population live in cramped slum communities and subsist as daily wage earners, social distancing and work-from-home arrangements are privileges reserved for the middle and upper classes of Philippine society" (Teehankee 2020). Poverty among Filipino families climbed as job losses and lost economic opportunities mounted, with 7.6 million Filipino households experiencing involuntary hunger as the economy contracted in 2020 by nearly 10 percent, the highest decline ever recorded (Arugelles 2021).

When assuming the presidency, Duterte had claimed to be a "socialist" open to social reform (Juego 2017; Mendoza 2018). He appointed four leftist cabinet members at the beginning of his administration when his administration was engaged in peace talks with the CPP. These progressives advocated a "Comprehensive Agreement on Social and Economic Reforms" of genuine land reform, including free land distribution, poverty reduction through universal social welfare programs, strict limits on mining, and other meaningful environmental regulations.

But Duterte's economic managers all "adhered to the free market, neoliberal economic framework of the previous administrations," with only token concessions to the progressive agenda (Casiño 2017; also Bello 2017; Putzel 2020; Ramos 2021). In fact, Duterte did not veer far from the neoliberal orthodoxy of his predecessors (Batalla 2016; Timberman 2019). Duterte's social policy initiatives either proved to be largely middle-class subsidies – free tuition in state higher education institutions to which few poor students have access. Or they were badly underfunded and largely unimplemented – universal health care to be financed by an insurance scheme tilted toward private medical care with no significant increase in public provision (Mendoza 2018; Punongbayan 2019a, 2019b). Rather, the Duterte government continued to rely largely on the CCT scheme which simply mitigated "some of the worst impacts of macroeconomic policies that have resulted in impoverishment, without inviting interrogation of the main development strategy that led to increased poverty in the first place" (Africa et al. 2017, 47). It had become clear that Duterte was "swinging to right-wing populism, in terms of discourse, governance style and his political support base" (Juego 2017, 134). When ceasefire talks broke down with the communists, Duterte quickly rid himself of his now unwanted leftist allies, criticizing them and their progressive policies.

Conclusion

Bello (2009, 3) speaks of the Philippines' "anti-development state" due to its "utter failure ... to deliver economic prosperity and reduce economic quality" which "is the greatest source of mass alienation." As this section has outlined, state neglect of the poor majority has been long in the making. Since the American colonial era, promises to "uplift" average Filipinos through agrarian reform have gone largely unfulfilled. Marcos' developmentalism was undermined by cronyism and debt-driven growth. Believing state-led strategies discredited, post-Marcos policymakers largely pursued neoliberal policies which generated growth. But it was highly unequal and did not result in robust gains in employment. As a result, the Philippines has by far the highest poverty incidence among the six major ASEAN economies, more than double Indonesia's, the next highest (ASEAN Secretariat 2019, 22). According the government's own estimates, the Philippines is expected to remain a laggard in its poverty rate in ASEAN through 2030 (M. Raquiza 2019, 18).

Duterte, like Marcos and Quezon before him, used the persistence of poverty to help justify democratic backsliding. "Proletarian populists" – Estrada, Poe, and Binay – who had attempted to turn class into a major political cleavage by promising to help the majority of Filipinos who consider themselves poor were overthrown, cheated, or subjected to selective investigation, respectively (Thompson 2008; Arugay and Slater 2019; Kenny 2020). Engaging largely in pseudo-social reform, Duterte emphasized his drug war as a silver bullet to the country's social problems. It proved popular across class lines although it hurt (and in fact disproportionately targeted and killed) the poor. The cross-class appeal of Duterte's drug war deflected from the real harm done by his brute force governance to the impoverished majority of the population.

5 Conclusion

This Element has situated the collapse of people power-inspired liberal reformism and democratic backsliding after the election of Duterte in 2016 – that appears to be continuing with the landslide victory of Marcos, Jr. in 2022 – within a larger structural crisis of Philippine democracy. But guided by a "structuration" perspective, it has also examined how Philippine presidents and elite "strategic groups" as key actors have been both constrained and enabled by oligarchical political structures and a highly unequal economy.

This authoritarian *Zeitgeist* in the Philippines has been blamed on conspiracy theories and attacks on "fake news" in the mainstream media propagated by pro-Duterte and pro-Marcos online communities (Talamayan 2019). Disinformation was an important aspect of Duterte's candidacy and presidency, as discussed in Section 3. Its "institutionalization" was significant in the spread of nostalgia for the authoritarian rule of Marcos, Sr., which is said to have "paved the way" for Marcos, Jr.'s easy victory in 2022 (Tuquero 2022; also see Ong and Cabañes 2018; Aguilar 2019; Talamayan 2021). A pro-Marcos commentator put forward a competing frame for understanding the impact of social media, claiming it broke "the Yellow's [the anti-Marcos forces] hegemony over Filipinos' minds through their control of mainstream media" (Tiglao 2022a). Recent research suggests misinformation reinforces rather than changes existing opinions (Allcott and Gentzkow 2017).

Yet Philippine democracy's discontents are not coterminous with the rise of social media. A "presentist" analysis of illiberalism focused on "tech determinism" benefits from broader historical perspective. This Element has suggested that the origins of the current crisis can be traced back to American colonial democracy and transgressive presidents, to reliance on political violence by strongman chief executives, and to the way in which mass poverty has been instrumentalized to justify regime change without actually undertaking serious efforts to improve the lot of impoverished Filipinos.

Three presidents – Quezon, Marcos, Sr. and Duterte – transgressed even the very limited constraints on executive power in a "hyper-presidential" system to backslide or destroy democracy, as discussed in Section 2. US colonial democracy established a model of patronage-driven politics with weak institutions. As Commonwealth president, Quezon monopolized patronage and advocated "partyless democracy." Only the advent of the Second World War preempted full-fledged authoritarian rule. Three decades later, Marcos declared martial law, dismantling electoral democracy and rights protection. Marcos could "not hide his contempt for liberal representative democracy," hoping to consign liberalism, an ideology of "foreign provenance," to the waste bin of Philippine history (Curaming 2020, 87).[12] Duterte's aggrandizement of power was even less subtle. He "slaughtered" Filipinos "by the thousands, justifying the murders by dismissing liberalism and human rights as 'Western'" (Claudio 2017a, 104).

Remigio E. Agpalo (1981) has influentially argued that Filipinos' organic–hierarchical worldview explains their cultural preference for paternalistic strongman leaders which he termed a "*pangulo* (head) regime," that is, the head of the body politic. For Agpalo, the "apogee" of this form of leadership was Marcos' martial law rule in which "Filipino identity had become whole and the body politic mutated into its most mature form" (Abinales 2017, 62). Contreras (2020, 55) argues that "Duterte is in fact a closer approximation to the 'pangulo' strongman than Marcos," accounting for much of former's charismatic appeal. Evidence from regional or world value surveys suggesting the majority of Filipinos have illiberal attitudes (Heydarian 2018, 6) underlines the plausibility of Agpalo's culturalist argument, although there is debate whether this is due to their fundamental illiberality (Pernia 2021) or to support for illiberal policies, not illiberalism generally (Kenny and Holmes 2020).

---

[12] Marcos launched a multivolume official history project called *Tadhana* (fate), employing some of the country's leading young historians, with the aim of providing historical culturalist justification for his authoritarian rule which could not however hide the fact that this academic effort was a "patently self-serving political project" (Curaming 2020, 87–88).

Yet as Section 2 also showed, other Filipino presidents have been "restorationist," attempting to stave off democratic regression or to restore democracy. In 1953, presidential candidate Magsaysay became the symbol of an elite political movement against the abuses of power by incumbent Quirino with the catchphrase "protect the ballot and save the nation." Backed by elite strategic groups and with strong support from the United States, Magsaysay won overwhelmingly and stabilized democracy. Nearly twenty years later, a similar elite coalition failed to stop Marcos from declaring martial law. But after only a little over a decade, the traditional opposition was able to mount huge protests after the Aquino assassination and ultimately toppled Marcos in people power. With a new constitution guaranteeing civil liberties and competitive elections, redemocratization began.

Agpalo (1996a) criticized Cory Aquino as a weak leader, the anti-thesis of Marcos, and inappropriate in the Philippine cultural–political context. But Agpalo (1996b, 167–168) also acknowledged liberal democracy has a long tradition in the Philippines, with the *ilustrados* (enlightened ones) fighting Spanish tyranny and demanding liberty for Filipinos. Jose Rizal's liberalism as well as liberal ideas and policies during the early post-war independence period have recently received renewed attention (Claudio 2017b, 2019). For a quarter century after people power, the "yellow" narrative appeared dominant, with its stress on the need to restore democracy and improve governance given the repression and corruption of Marcos' authoritarianism. Cory Aquino was a much loved leader and her funeral in 2009, as discussed in the Introduction, was a moment of national mourning. But during the Noynoy Aquino presidency, the hollowing out of the liberal reformist project through the scandals and weak institutions typical of a patronage-driven system created a political opportunity seized by Duterte to revert to strongman rule.

The local origins of Duterte's violent populist political messaging which won him the presidency in 2016 and made him the most popular president to date were discussed in Section 3. All three forms of political violence – rebellion, anti-insurgency, and warlordism – were rampant in Davao where Duterte became mayor in 1988. Mixing these elements, Duterte conjured up a strategy of neo-bossism. He triangulated between insurgent groups and the armed forces while hiring former rebels and soldiers to form a warlord army that became known as the Davao Death Squad to target small-time drug users and dealers. Duterte also later turned on his once leftist allies after the breakdown of peace talks with the CPP, passing an "Anti-Terrorism" law that has seen the rise in the extrajudicial killings of activists linked to the communists but engaged in legal activities in cities, not in armed struggle in a rural-based insurgency. Duterte's signature "war on drugs" and his later targeting of legal leftists was akin to previous chief executives' reliance on political violence, particularly by Marcos Sr., even during his pre-martial law presidency, and by Quirino in the early independence period.

For nearly a century, Philippine presidents have been adept at both decrying, and deflecting from grave social inequality, as analyzed in Section 4. Precedent setting was the failure to fairly redistribute the friar estates during the early American colonial period. Social reform proposals often came in reaction to growing peasant-based insurgencies (particularly during Quezon's, Magsaysay's, and Marcos' presidencies). They were also meant to demonstrate that a progressive era was replacing a reactionary order: American colonialism followed the Spanish "dark ages"; Marcos repudiated the old oligarchical order in favor of his "New Society"; and post-people power politicians promised good governance through market-oriented reforms after a disastrous dictatorship had discredited state-led developmentalism. Yet, in the end, expectations of inclusive growth and significant social reforms have been repeatedly disappointed.

Like previous promises and programs, the drug crackdown was also offered as a solution to, and misdirected from persistent poverty. Duterte demonized small-time drug users and dealers (and hardheaded *pasaway* during the COVID-19 pandemic) as holding back Philippine development, offering the draconian solution of "order over law" (Pepinsky 2017). As a legitimation strategy, extravagant but largely empty promises of enacting social reform, ending corruption, and eradicating illegal drugs have proved remarkably effective political tools. Despite the Philippines being among the worst pandemic performers globally (Bloomberg 2021; Sarao 2021), Duterte's approval ratings remained robust. His "brute force governance" involving personalized strongman rule, blame-shifting, and securitization undermined the dynamics of accountability. This enabled him to win public approval despite the failure of both the drug war to actually reduce substance abuse and widespread lockdowns to curb the spread of the pandemic (Thompson 2022b).

Duterte's popularity created strong political demand for a presidential candidate with a similar strongman image, with surveys showing 85 percent of Filipinos preferring "partial" or even "full continuity" to his rule (Arguelles 2022). Ferdinand Romualdez Marcos, Jr., the son of the "conjugal" dictatorship couple of Imelda Romualdez and Ferdinand Marcos, Sr. who ran on the revisionist claim that his parents' rule represented a "golden age" in the country's politics, easily won the May 2022 presidential elections (Mijares 1976; Tuquero 2022). Yet this appeal must be understood within the larger context of democratic ambivalence in which voters' support for democracy is conditional, with an increasing openness to authoritarian governance (Webb 2017; Garrido 2022). With a slogan of "unity," Marcos, Jr. ran with Duterte's daughter, Sara "Inday" Duterte-Carpio, as his vice presidential candidate. She won by even a greater margin than he did in separate elections for the number two spot. The Marcos–Duterte tandem had successfully positioned themselves as the rightful heirs to Duterte's legacy (Arguelles 2022).

Marcos, Jr. has, as of this writing, downplayed the drug war, though drug killings have continued despite a supposed revamping to emphasize rehabilitation (Vera Files 2022). He has also emphasized the need for rapid post-pandemic recovery amidst high inflation and enhanced social welfare, including traditional pledges to improve the lot of farmers and even vague promises of renewed land reform (Aning 2022; PCIJ Staff 2022). His public statements, particularly about enforcing a UN tribunal's ruling that backed the Philippines' claims in the South China Sea, also suggest he is prepared to reverse Duterte's illiberal realignment toward China.[13] Yet there is little indication he intends to change his predecessor's illiberal course. Critical media remains under threat with the online newspaper *Rappler*, led by Nobel Peace Prize winner Maria Ressa, facing a court-ordered shutdown (Yap and Calonzo 2022), a prominent historian has been accused of bias against the Marcoses (Bernardo 2022), and the Marcos government has rejected a proposal to rejoin the ICC which the Philippines left after it began investigating Duterte's drug war (Mercado 2022).

Yet, as discussed in Section 2, the Philippines has also had past examples of democratic renaissance – during the early independence period when Magsaysay's victory as president staved off potential autocratization and after Marcos' dictatorship was toppled by "people power" in 1986. With its discourse of redemocratization and the restoration of good governance, resurgent opposition was led by powerful elite strategic groups. However, after the recent return to autocratization, the country has reached a democratic nadir. Ordonez and Borja (2018) have argued that the Philippines under Duterte became a paradigmatic case of the separation of popular legitimacy from liberal rights that Mounk (2018) identified as the chief characteristic of illiberal populism, to which Duterte has added his own murderous methods (Thompson 2022a). Even Kenny and Holmes' (2020) narrower argument that it was not that the majority of Filipino voters had necessarily become illiberal but rather that they were

---

[13] Illiberal realignment as part of Duterte's effort to defend the drug war against criticisms from the United States and Europe was limited by the logic of hedging between China and the West (Suorsa and Thompson 2018). Despite his often fiery anti-colonialism–inspired rhetoric against the United States, Duterte ultimately did not make major changes in Philippines' relationship with the American government. Crucially, under pressure from his own military, he reaffirmed the US visiting forces agreement. But Marcos, Jr.'s apparent support for the Permanent Court of Arbitration's ruling under the United Nations Convention on the Law of the Sea overturning the latter's "nine dash line" claim that involved Philippine territory in the South China Sea (which the Philippines terms the West Philippine Sea) does seem a significant discursive shift as Duterte had soft-pedalled the issue (Wong 2022).

supportive of certain illiberal policies led them to conclude that "Duterte has clearly utilized the overwhelming popularity of his war on drugs to assault already severely damaged political institutions, from the legislature to the judiciary to the media" (Holmes 2020, 202).

Despite the highly illiberal nature of Duterte's rule, particularly the drug war, he continued to claim democratic legitimacy based on competitive elections and high opinion poll ratings while ruling largely constitutionally. This undermined electoral opposition and weakened pushback by critical Catholic bishops, big business groups, and civil society activists, with no sustained protests and the "yellows" out-"trolled" on social media (Thompson 2021). Among the major strategic groups in the Philippines, the military alone remained a significant check on Duterte (Quimpo 2021).

Moreover, as discussed in Section 2, the "people power" narrative was gradually discredited, making the opposition's overwhelming defeat in the 2022 elections by Marcos, Jr. particularly poignant. He was their *bête noire* given his presidential campaign was based on authoritarian nostalgia for his father's rule which they had long used as a foil for their own democratic credentials and promises of improving governance. This demonstrated how unappealing this discourse had become for most Filipinos. With its recent democratic backsliding, the Philippines is an object lesson in the failure of a liberal reformist project to improve the lot of ordinary people as well as substantially reshape the political system to lessen dependence on patronage, strengthen institutions, and reduce political violence.

References

Abinales, P. N. 1996. When a Revolution Devours Its Children before Victory: *Operasyon Kampanyang Ahos* and the Tragedy of Mindanao Communism. In P. N. Abinales, ed., *The Revolution Falters: The Left in Philippine Politics after 1986*. Ithaca: Cornell University, 154–179.

2015. Digong's Mouth. *Rappler* (December 6): www.rappler.com/thought-leaders/115071-duterte-mouth-censorship/.

2017. Political Science and the Marcos Dictatorship. *Social Transformations Journal of the Global South* (April): https://ajolbeta.ateneo.edu/stjgs/articles/93/1118.

Abinales, P. N. & D. J. Amoroso. 2017. *State and Society in the Philippines, Second Edition*. Lanham: Rowman and Littlefield.

Abueva, J. V. 1971. *Ramon Magsaysay: A Political Biography*. Manila: Solidaridad.

Africa, J., M. Raquiza, E. Ursua & E. Jimenez. 2017. *Reforming Philippine Poverty Policy*. Quezon City: National Anti-Poverty Commission.

Agpalo, R. E. 1981. The Philippines: From Communal to Societal Pangulo Regime. *Philippine Law Journal* 56(1): 56–98.

1996a. Leadership and Types of Filipino Leaders: Focus on Ferdinand E. Marcos and Corazon C. Aquino. In R. E. Agpalo, ed., *Adventures in Political Science*. Quezon City: University of the Philippines Press, 251–269.

1996b. The Organic-Hierarchical Paradigm and Politics in the Philippines. In R. E. Agpalo, ed., *Adventures in Political Science*. Quezon City: University of the Philippines Press, 163–194.

Agojo K. N. M. 2021. Policing a Pandemic: Understanding the State and Political Instrumentalization of the Coercive Apparatus in Duterte's Philippines. *Journal of Developing Societies* 37(3), 363–386.

Aguilar, F. V. 2019. Political Conjuncture and Scholarly Disjunctures: Reflections on Studies of the Philippine State under Marcos. *Philippine Studies: Historical and Ethnographic Viewpoints* 67(1), 3–30.

Aim, S. 2016. How Duterte Won the Election on Facebook. *New Mandala* (May 12): www.newmandala.org/how-dutertewon-the-election-on-facebook/.

Albert, J. R. G., J. C. Dumagan & A. Martinez, Jr. 2015. Inequalities in Income, Labor and Education: The Challenges of Inclusive Growth. *Philippine Institute of Development Studies*, Discussion Paper Series No. 2015–2001.

Allcott, H. & M. Gentzkow. 2017. Social Media and Fake News in the 2016 Election. *Journal of Economic Perspectives* 31(2), 211–236.

Allard, T. & K. Lema. 2020. Exclusive: "Shock and Awe" has Failed in Philippines' Drug War, Enforcement Chief Says. *Reuters* (February 7): www.reuters.com/article/us-philippines-drugs-performance-exclusi-idUSKBN2010IL.

Amnesty International. 2019. "They Just Kill": Ongoing Extrajudicial Executions and Other Violations in the Philippines' "War on Drugs." Amnesty International: www.justice.gov/eoir/page/file/1180791/download.

Anderson, B. 1988. Cacique Democracy in the Philippines: Origins and Dreams. *New Left Review* I/169, 3–31.

Aning, J. 2022. Bongbong Marcos' First SONA: It's All About Economy. *Philippine Daily Inquirer* (July 25): https://newsinfo.inquirer.net/1633568/marcos-first-sona-its-all-about-economy#ixzz7a8h8EXbK.

Arcellana, E. Y. 1961. Quezon's Gift: A Dream of Social Justice: "Not for a Few Alone, but for All, Especially the Poor." *Philippines Free Press* (August 19): https://philippinesfreepress.wordpress.com/1961/08/19/quezons-gift-a-dream-of-social-justice-august-19–1961/.

Arguelles, C. V. 2019. "We Are Rodrigo Duterte": Dimensions of the Philippine Populist Publics' Vote. *Asian Politics & Policy* 11(3), 417–437.

2021. The Populist Brand Is Crisis: Durable Dutertismo Amidst Mismanaged COVID-19 Response. In Daljit Singh and Malcolm Cook, eds., *Southeast Asian Affairs*, 257–274.

2022. The Triumph of the Marcos-Duterte Leviathan. *The Medium* (May 10): https://medium.com/@clevearguelles/the-triumph-of-the-marcos-duterte-leviathan-f8b8165b9759.

Arugay A. A. & D. Slater. 2019. Polarization without Poles: Machiavellian Conflicts and the Philippines' Lost Decade of Democracy, 2000–2010. *The ANNALS of the American Academy of Political and Social Science* 681(1), 122–136.

Arguillas, C. 2011. Maguindanao: The Long Shadow of the Ampatuans. In Y. Chua & L. Rimban, eds., *Democracy at Gunpoint: Election-Related Violence in the Philippines*. Makati: The Asia Foundation, 1–26.

ASEAN Secretariat. 2019. *ASEAN Key Figures 2019*. Jakarta: The ASEAN Secretariat.

Asian Development Bank. 2005. *Poverty in the Philippines: Income, Assets and Access*. Manila: Asian Development Bank.

Aspinall, E. & M. Mietzner. 2019. Southeast Asia's Troubling Elections: Nondemocratic Pluralism in Indonesia. *Journal of Democracy* 30(4), 104–118.

Balisacan, A. M. 2001. Did the Estrada Administration Benefit the Poor? In A. Doronila & J. V. Abueva, eds., *Between Fires: Fifteen Perspectives on the Estrada Crisis*. Pasig: Anvil, 98–112.

Barry, C. 2006. The Limits of Conservative Church Reformism in the Democratic Philippines. In T. Cheng & D. Brown, eds., *Religious Organizations and Democratization: Case Studies from Contemporary Asia*. Armonk: M.E. Sharpe, 157–179.

Batalla, E. V. C. 2016. Divided Politics and Economic Growth in the Philippines. *Journal of Current Southeast Asian Affairs* 35(3), 161–186.

Batalla, E. V. C., M. Sta. Romana & K. Rodrigo. 2018. The Judiciary under Threat. In M. R. Thompson & E. V. C. Batalla, eds., *Handbook of the Contemporary Philippines*. London: Routledge, 107–117.

Bautista, G. M. 2003. An Assessment of the Philippine Economy. *Kyoto Review of Southeast Asia* 4 (October): https://kyotoreview.org/issue-4/an-assessment-of-the-philippine-economy/.

Beissinger, M. 2007. Structure and Example in Modular Political Phenomena: The Diffusion of Bulldozer/Rose/Orange/Tulip Revolutions. *Perspectives on Politics* 5(2), 259–276.

Bello, W. 2009. *The Anti-Development State: The Political Economy of Permanent Crisis in the Philippines*. London: Zen Books.

    2016. The Left under Duterte. *Jacobin* (August 7): www.jacobinmag.com/2016/06/walden-bello-philippines-duterte-dignidad-coalition-akbayan/.

    2017. Why It's Time for Progressives in the Duterte Cabinet to Leave. *Rappler* (August 20): www.rappler.com/thought-leaders/179285-time-progressives-duterte-cabinet-leave-drug-war-killings.

    2019. Duterte's Revolt against Liberal Democracy. *Global Dialogue* 8(3): https://globaldialogue.isa-sociology.org/dutertes-revolt-against-liberal-democracy/.

Beltran, M. 2020. In the Philippines, a Label Can Take Your Life: Accusation as a Communist – "Red-Tagging" – Is a Potential Death Sentence, Which Doesn't Stop Some from Using It. *The Interpreter* (December 3): www.lowyinstitute.org/the-interpreter/philippines-label-can-take-your-life.

Berlin, D. L. 1982. Prelude to Martial Law: An Examination of Pre-1972 Philippine Civil-Military Relations. PhD dissertation, University of South Carolina.

Bernardo, J. 2022. Academics Defend Historian Ambeth Ocampo vs. "Smear Campaign." *ABS-CBN News* (July 11): https://news.abs-cbn.com/news/07/11/22/history-is-not-gossip-academics-defend-historian-ambeth-ocampo.

Berner, E. 2001. Kollektive Strategien, Herrschaft und Widerstand: Zur Relevanz einer Theorie strategischer Gruppen in der Entwicklungssoziologie. In H. Schrader, M. Kaiser & R. Korff, eds., *Markt, Kultur, Gesellschaft: Zur Aktualität von 25 Jahren Entwicklungsforschung*. Münster: LIT Verlag, 113–132.

Bermeo, N. 2016. On Democratic Backsliding. *Journal of Democracy* 27(1), 5–19.

Bloomberg. 2021. The Covid Resilience Ranking: The Best and Worst Places to Be as We Learn to Live with Delta. *Bloomberg* (September 28): www .bloomberg.com/graphics/covid-resilience-ranking/.

Bolongaita Jr., E. P. 1995. Presidential versus Parliamentary Democracy. *Philippine Studies: Historical and Ethnographic Viewpoints* 43, 105–123.

Bonner, R. 1987. *Waltzing with a Dictator: The Marcoses and the Making of American Policy*. New York: Times Books.

Borras, S. M. 2007. *Pro-Poor Land Reform: A Critique*. Ottawa: University of Ottawa Press.

Brillantes, A. B. 1987. *Dictatorship and Martial Law: Philippine Authoritarianism in 1972*. Manila: Great Books.

Boudreau, V. 2009. Elections, Repression and Authoritarian Survival in Post-Transition Indonesia and the Philippines. *The Pacific Review* 22(2), 223–253.

Boyce, J. K. 1993. *The Political Economy of Growth and Impoverishment in the Marcos Era*. Quezon City: Ateneo de Manila Press.

Cabañes, J. & J. Cornelio. 2017. The Rise of Trolls in the Philippines (and What We Can Do about It). In N. Curato, ed., *A Duterte Reader: Critical Essays on Rodrigo Duterte's Early Presidency*. Quezon City: Ateneo de Manila Press, 231–250.

Casiño, T. 2017. Duterte's Falling Out with the Left. *Rappler* (Sept. 9, 2017): www.rappler.com/voices/thought-leaders/duterte-falling-out-left.

Castañeda Anastacio, L. 2016. *The Foundations of the Modern Philippine State: Imperial Rule and the American Constitutional Tradition in the Philippine Islands, 1898–1935*. Cambridge: Cambridge University Press.

Claudio, L. E. 2013. *Taming People's Power: The Edsa Revolutions and Their Contradictions*. Quezon City: Ateneo de Manila University Press.

    2017a. Defending Liberalism in the Global South: Notes from Duterte's Philippines. *The Global South* 11(2), 92–107.

    2017b. *Liberalism and the Postcolony: Thinking the State in 20th-Century Philippines*. Singapore: National University of Singapore Press.

    2019. *Jose Rizal: Liberalism and the Paradox of Coloniality*. London: Palgrave.

Claudio, L. E. & P. N. Abinales. 2017. Dutertismo, Maoismo, Nasyonalismo. In N. Curato, ed., *A Duterte Reader: Critical Essays on Rodrigo Duterte's Early Presidency*. Quezon City: Ateneo de Manila Press, 93–110.

Collier, K. 1995. Bringing Civil Society Back In: Rectification in the Philippine Revolutionary Movement and the Idiom of Resistance in Davao. *South East Asia Research* 3(1), 92–119.

Collins, J. 2016a. Development First: Multilateralism in the Post-"War on Drugs" Era. In *After the Drug Wars: Report of the LSE Expert Group on the Economics of Drug Policy.* London: London School of Economics, 9–18: https://www.lse .ac.uk/ideas/Assets/Documents/reports/LSE-IDEAS-After-Drug-Wars.pdf.

2016b. Why the Philippines' New War on Drug Users Will Fail. *Business World Online* (August 2): www.bworld.online.com/content.php?section= Opinion&title=why-the-philippines-new-war-on-drug-users-will-fail&id= 131265.

Combinido, P. 2019. When Illiberal Social Media Takes Over Democratic Philippines. *New Mandala* (February 6): www.newmandala.org/when-illiberal-social-media-takes-over-democratic-philippines/.

Combinido, P. & N. Curato. 2021. Curing "Patient Zero": Reclaiming the Digital Public Sphere in the Philippines. In S. Aim & R. Tapsell, eds., *From Grassroots Activism to Disinformation: Social Media in Southeast Asia.* Singapore: ISEAS, 19–42.

Contreras, A. P. 2020. Rodrigo Duterte as Ideology: Academic vs. Social Media Myths and Representations and Their Implications to Political Order. *Philippine Political Science Journal* 41, 48–72.

Corpus, V. N. 1989. *The Silent War.* Quezon City: VNC Enterprises.

Coronel, S. 2017. Are Priests Duterte's Fiercest Foes? *The New York Times* (August 4): www.nytimes.com/2017/08/04/opinion/are-priests-dutertes-fiercest-foes.html.

Crispin, S. W. 2018. Duterte Leads Tri-Pronged Attack on Press Amid Condemnation of Controversial Policies. *Committee for the Protection of Journalists* (July 5): https://cpj.org/blog/2018/07/mission-journal-duterte-leads-tri-pronged-attack-o.php.

Curaming, R. A. 2020. *Power and Knowledge in Southeast Asia: State and Scholars in Indonesia and the Philippines.* London: Routledge.

Curato, N. 2016. Politics of Anxiety, Politics of Hope: Penal Populism and Duterte's Rise to Power. *Journal of Current Southeast Asian Affairs* 35(3), 91–109.

2017. Flirting with Authoritarian Fantasies? Rodrigo Duterte and the New Terms of Philippine Populism. *Journal of Contemporary Asia* 47(1), 142–153.

2021. Democratic Expressions amidst Fragile Institutions: Possibilities for Reform in Duterte's Philippines. *Democracy in Asia* (January 22): www .brookings.edu/articles/democratic-expressions-amidst-fragile-institutions-possibilities-for-reform-in-dutertes-philippines/.

2022. The Return of a Marcos to Power in the Philippines Is a Warning to the World. *The Guardian* (May 18): www.theguardian.com.

Curato, N. & J. Ong. 2018. Who Laughs at a Rape Joke? Illiberal Responsiveness in Rodrigo Duterte. University of Massachusetts Amherst, ScholarWorks@UMass Amherst, Communication Department Faculty Publication: https://scholarworks.umass.edu/cgi/viewcontent.cgi?article=1064&context=communication_faculty_pubs.

Dañguilan, M. 2018. *The RH Bill Story: Contentions and Compromises.* Quezon City: Ateneo de Manila Press.

David, R. 2016. Dutertismo. *Philippine Daily Inquirer* (May 1): https://opinion.inquirer.net/94530/dutertismo.

de Dios, E. S. & P. D. Hutchroft. 2003. Political Economy. In A. M. Balisacan & H. Hill, eds., *The Philippine Economy: Development, Policies, and Challenges.* Quezon City: Ateneo de Manila University Press, 45–73.

Deinla, I., V. Taylor & S. Rood. 2018. Philippines: Justice Removed, Justice Denied. *The Interpreter* (May 17): www.lowyinstitute.org/the-interpreter/philippines-justice-removed-justice-denied.

Dohner, R. S. & P. Intal, Jr. 1989. The Marcos Legacy: Economic Policy and Foreign Debt in the Philippine. In J. D. Sachs & S. M. Collins, eds., *Developing Country Debt and Economic Performance, vol. 3: Country Studies – Indonesia, Korea, Philippines, Turkey.* Chicago: University of Chicago Press, 373–400.

Doronila, A. 1985. The Transformation of Patron-Client Relations and Its Political Consequences in Postwar Philippines. *Journal of Southeast Asian Studies* 16(1), 99–116.

Dreisbach, J. 2018. Social Media and Blogging: The Changing Philippine Media Landscape under the Duterte Regime. *Kyoto Review of Southeast Asia* (August 23): https://kyotoreview.org/yav/social-media-blogging-under-duterte-regime/.

Dressel, B. & C. R. Bonoan. 2019. Southeast Asia's Troubling Elections: Duterte versus the Rule of Law. *Journal of Democracy* 30(4), 134–148.

Evangelista, R. E. 2015. Who Were Really behind Makati's Yellow Confetti Rallies? *Rappler* (September 24): www.rappler.com/moveph/106976-makati-confetti-rallies-marcos/.

Evers, H.-D. 1973. Group Conflict and Class Formation in South-East Asia. In H.-D. Evers, ed., *Modernization in South-East Asia.* Singapore: Oxford University Press, 108–131

Evers, H.-D., T. Schiel & R. Korff. 1988. *Strategische Gruppen: Vergleichende Studien zu Staat, Bürokratie und Klassenbildung in der Dritten Welt.* Berlin: D. Reimer.

Evers, H.-D. & S. Gerke. 2008. Strategic Group Analysis. Center for Development, Bonn: Bonn University (November 9).

Fegan, B. 1979. Folk-Capitalism: Economic Strategies of Peasants in a Philippine Wet-Rice Village. PhD dissertation, Yale University.

Fernandez, G. M. 2021. Rise of Illiberal Democracy, Weakening of the Rule of Law, & Implementation of Human Rights in the Philippines. *American University International Law Review* 36(2): https://digitalcommons.wcl.american.edu/cgi/viewcontent.cgi?article=2061 &context=auilr.

Ferrara, F. 2015. *The Political Development of Modern Thailand*. Cambridge: Cambridge University Press.

Franco, J. & P. Abinales. 2007. Again, They're Killing Peasants in the Philippines – Lawlessness, Murder and Impunity. *Critical Asian Studies* 39(2), 315–328.

Garcia, M. G. 2005. The "Spanish Colonial Past" in the Construction of Modern Philippine History: A Critical Inquiry into the (Mis)use of Spanish Sources. PhD dissertation, National University of Singapore: https://core.ac.uk/download/pdf/48645937.pdf.

Garrido, M. 2022. The Ground for the Illiberal Turn in the Philippines. *Democratization* 29(4), 673–691.

Gavilan, J. & R. Talabong. 2020. Policing a Pandemic: Philippines Still Stuck with Drug War Blueprint. *Rappler* (May 1): www.rappler.com/newsbreak/in-depth/policing-coronavirus-pandemic-philippines-still-stuck-drug-war-blueprint.

Gera, W. 2020. Heightened Contradictions: Duterte and Local Autonomy in the Era of COVID-19. *New Mandala* (June 5): www.newmandala.org/heightened-contradictions-duterte-and-local-autonomy-in-the-era-of-covid-1/.

Gera, W. & P. D. Hutchcroft. 2021. Duterte's Tight Grip over Local Politicians: Can it Endure? *New Mandala* (February 19): www.newmandala.org/dutertes-tight-grip-over-local-politicians-can-it-endure/.

Giddens, A. 1984. *The Constitution of Society: Outline of the Theory of Structuration*. Cambridge: Polity Press.

Gomez, B. 2015. Murder Most Foul: Marcos' Youthful Exuberance. *ABS-CBN News* (September 9): https://news.abs-cbn.com/blogs/opinions/09/09/15/murder-most-foul-marcos-youthful-exuberance.

Guerrero, L. M. 1938. Juan Sumulong: Dreamer, Not Demagogue. *Philippines Free Press* (September 17): https://philippinesfreepress.wordpress.com/tag/juan-sumulong/.

Gutierrez, J. 2021. Ex-Mayor on Duterte's "Narco Politician" List Is Killed. *New York Times* (June 17): www.nytimes.com/2021/06/17/world/asia/philippines-mayor-dead-drugs.html.

Habito, C. 2013. Inequity, Initiative and Inclusive Growth. *Philippine Daily Inquirer* (March 11): http://opinion.inquirer.net/48623/inequity-initiative-and-inclusive- growth.

Haggard, S. 2018. *Developmental States.* Cambridge: Cambridge University Press.

Hapal K. 2021. The Philippines' COVID-19 Response: Securitising the Pandemic and Disciplining the Pasaway. *Journal of Current Southeast Asian Affairs* 40(2), 224–244.

Hau, C. S. 2016. What Is Crony Capitalism? *Emerging State Project* (April 8). Tokyo: National Graduate Institute for Policy Studies: www3.grips.ac.jp/~esp/en/event/what-is-%E2%80%9Ccrony-capitalism%E2%80%9D/index.html.

Hayami, Y., A. R. Quisumbing & L. S. Andriano. 1990. *Toward an Alternative Land Reform Paradigm: A Philippine Perspective*. Quezon City: Ateneo de Manila University Press.

Hedman, E.-L. E. 2001. The Spectre of Populism in Philippine Politics and Society: Artista, Masa, Eraption! *South East Asia Research* 9(1), 5–44.

2006. *In the Name of Civil Society: From Free Election Movements to People Power in the Philippines*. Honolulu: University of Hawaii Press.

Hedman, E.-L. E. & J. T. Sidel. 2000. *Philippine Politics and Society in the Twentieth Century: Colonial Legacies, Post-Colonial Trajectories*. London: Routledge.

Heydarian, R. J. 2018. *The Rise of Duterte: A Populist Revolt against Elite Democracy*. London: Palgrave.

Hodder, R. 2018. The Civil Service. In M. R. Thompson & E. V. C. Batalla, eds., *Routledge Handbook of the Contemporary Philippines*. London: Routledge, 73–84.

Holmes, R. 2016. The Dark Side of Electoralism: Opinion Polls and Voting in the 2016 Philippine Presidential Election. *Journal of Current Southeast Asian Affairs* 35(3), 15–38.

Holmes, R. 2018. Pork Transmorgified: The Unending Story of Particularistic Spending in the Philippines. In M. R. Thompson & E. V. C. Batalla, eds., *Routledge Handbook of the Contemporary Philippines*. London: Routledge, 97–106.

Human Rights Watch. 2009. "You Can Die Any Time": Philippines – Dismantle "Davao Death Squad" (April 6): www.hrw.org/report/2009/04/06/you-can-die-any-time/death-squad-killings-mindanao.

Hutchcroft, P. D. 1998 *Booty Capitalism: The Politics of Banking in the Philippines*. Ithaca: Cornell University Press.

2008. The Arroyo Imbroglio in the Philippines. *Journal of Democracy* 19(1), 141–155.

2011. Reflections on a Reverse Image: South Korea under Park Chung Hee and the Philippines under Ferdinand Marcos. In B.-K. Kim & E. F. Vogel, eds., *The Park Chung Hee Era: The Transformation of South Korea*. Cambridge, MA: Harvard University Press, 542–572.

2019. Midterm Elections Deepen Duterte's Domination. *East Asia Forum* (June 2): www.eastasiaforum.org/2019/06/02/midterm-elections-deepen-dutertes-domination/.

Hutchcroft, P. D. & W. Gera. 2022. Strong-Arming, Weak Steering: Central-Local Relations in the Philippines in the Era of the Pandemic. *Philippine Political Science Journal* 43(2), 123–167.

Hutchcroft, P. D. & R. D. Holmes. 2020. A Failure of Execution. *Inside Story* (April 4): https://insidestory.org.au/a-failure-of-execution/.

Iglesias, S. 2018. Central-Local Dynamics and Political Violence in the Philippines, 2001–2016. PhD dissertation, National University of Singapore.

Institute for Autonomy and Development. 2015. Did You Know? Cost of War in Mindanao? *Shaping Public Policy for Peace and Governance* (April 6): https://iag.org.ph/news/548-did-you-know-cost-of-war-in-mindanao.

Janjira S. & A. Arugay. 2016. Duterte's War on Drugs: Bitter Lessons from Thailand's Failed Campaign. *The Conversation* (September 26): https://theconversation.com/dutertes-war-on-drugs-bitter-lessons-from-thailands-failed-campaign-66096.

Jensen, S. & K. Hapal. 2018. Police Violence and Corruption in the Philippines: Violent Exchange and the War on Drugs. *Journal of Current Southeast Asian Affairs* 37(2), 39–62.

Jimenez, J. V. 2020. Ensuring American Control over the Philippine Economy through the Imposition of the Parity Rights. DLSU Research Congress 2020 (June 17–19): www.dlsu.edu.ph/wp-content/uploads/pdf/conferences/research-congress-proceedings/2020/TPH-09.pdf.

Johnson, D. T. & J. Fernquest. 2018. Governing through Killing: The War on Drugs in the Philippines. *Asian Journal of Law and Society* 5(2), 359–390.

Jones, G. R. 1989. *Red Revolution: Inside the Philippine Guerrilla Movement*. Boulder: Westview.

Judis, J. 2016. *The Populist Explosion: How the Great Recession Transformed American and European Politics*. New York: Columbia University Press.

Juego, B. 2017. The Philippines 2017: Duterte-Led Authoritarian Populism and Its Liberal Democratic Roots. *Asia Maior* 28, 129–163.

Kane, J. 2009. *The Politics of Moral Capital*. Cambridge: Cambridge University Press.

Kang, D. C. 2002. *Crony Capitalism: Corruption and Development in South Korea and the Philippines*. Cambridge: Cambridge University Press.

Kasuya, Y. 2009. *Presidential Bandwagon: Parties and Party Systems in the Philippines*. Pasig City: Anvil.

Kasuya, Y. & J. Teehankee. 2020. Duterte Presidency and the 2019 Midterm Election: An Anarchy of Parties? *Philippine Political Science Journal* 41 (12), 106–126.

Keenan, J. 2013. The Grim Reality Behind the Philippines' Economic Growth. *The Atlantic* (May 7): www.theatlantic.com/international/archive/2013/05/the-grim-reality-behind-the-philippines-economic-growth/275597/.

Kenny, P. 2020. Why Is There No Political Polarization in the Philippines? *Carnegie Endowment for International Peace* (August 18): https://carnegieendowment.org/2020/08/18/why-is-there-no-political-polarization-in-philippines-pub-82439.

Kenny, P. & R. Holmes. 2020. A New Penal Populism? Rodrigo Duterte, Public Opinion, and the War on Drugs in the Philippines. *Journal of East Asian Studies* 20(2), 187–205.

Kerkvliet, B. J. T. 1977. *The Huk Rebellion: A Study of Peasant Revolt in the Philippines*. Berkeley: University of California Press.

Kessler, R. J. 1989. *Rebellion and Repression in the Philippines*. New Haven: Yale University Press.

Kho, K. R. G. 2019. Behavioural Biases and Identity in Social Media: The Case of Philippine Populism, President Duterte's Rise, and Ways Forward. *Lee Kwan Yew School of Public Policy, National University of Singapore*: https://lkyspp.nus.edu.sg/docs/default-source/case-studies/behavioural-biases-and-identity-in-social-media_1204.pdf?sfvrsn=d3f77a0a_2.

Kimura, M. 2018. Clientelism Revisited. In M. R. Thompson & E. V. C. Batalla, eds., *Routledge Handbook of the Contemporary Philippines*. London: Routledge, 17–25.

King, R. 1977. *Land Reform: A World Survey*. Boulder: Westview Press.

Kirsch, H. & C. Welzel. 2019. Democracy Misunderstood: Authoritarian Notions of Democracy around the Globe. *Social Forces* 98(1), 59–92.

Kreuzer, P. 2016. "If They Resist, Kill Them All": Police Vigilantism in the Philippines. Frankfurt am Main: Peace Research Institute Frankfurt PRIF Report No. 142: www.hsfk.de/fileadmin/HSFK/hsfk_publikationen/prif142.pdf.

    2020. Governors and Mayors in the Philippines: Resistance to or Support for Duterte's Deadly War on Drugs. Peace Research Institute (PRIF) Report, Frankfurt am Main: Hessische Stiftung Friedens- und Konfliktforschung: https://nbnresolving.org/urn:nbn:de:0168-ssoar-71309-0.

Kulkarni, V. G. & R. Tasker. 1996. Promises to Keep. *Far Eastern Economic Review* (February 29), 22.

Kuntz, P. & M. R. Thompson. 2009. More than the Final Straw: Stolen Elections as Revolutionary Triggers. *Comparative Politics* 41(3), 253–272.

Kusaka, W. 2017. Bandit Grabbed the State: Duterte's Moral Politics. *Philippine Sociological Review* 65, 40–75.

Ileto, R. C. 1985. The Past in the Present Crisis. In R. J. May & Francisco Nemenzo, eds., *The Philippines after Marcos*. London: Croom Helm, 10–22.

Landé, C. H. 1965. *Leaders, Factions, and Parties: The Structure of Philippine Politics*. New Haven: Southeast Asian Studies, Yale University.

   1996. *Post-Marcos Politics: A Geographic and Statistical Analysis of the 1992 Philippine Elections*. Singapore: ISEAS.

   2001. The Return of "People Power" in the Philippines. *Journal of Democracy* 12(2), 88–102.

Lansdale, E. G. 1972. *In the Midst of Wars*. New York: Harper & Row.

Lasco, G. 2016. Just How Big Is the Drug Problem in the Philippines Anyway? *The Conversation* (October 13): https://theconversation.com/just-how-big-is-the-drug-problem-in-the-philippines-anyway-66640.

   2017. Inside the Philippines' Long Journey towards Reproductive Health. *The Conversation* (May 9): https://theconversation.com/inside-the-philippines-long-journey-towards-reproductive-health-72737.

   2020a. The "*Pasaway*" as Scapegoat. *Philippine Daily Inquirer* (April 30): https://opinion.inquirer.net/129356/the-pasaway-as-scapegoat.

   2020b. Medical Populism and the COVID-19 Pandemic. *Global Public Health* 15(10), 1417–1429.

Linantud, J. 1998. Whither Guns, Goons, and Gold? The Decline of Factional Election Violence in the Philippines. *Contemporary Southeast Asia* 20(3), 298–318.

Linz, J. J. 2000 [1975]. *Totalitarian and Authoritarian Regimes*. Boulder: Lynne Rienner.

Lucero, V. & M. Mangahas. 2016. Big Kill of Small Fry, Puny Drugs Haul, Defies PNP Rules. *Philippine Center for Investigative Journalism* (July 25): http://pcij.org/uncategorized/big-kill-of-small-fry-puny-drugs-haul-defies-pnp-rules/.

Luton, H. 1971. American Internal Revenue Policy in the Philippines to 1916. In N. G. Owen, ed., *Compadre Colonialism: Studies on the Philippines under American Rule*. Ann Arbor: Center for South and Southeast Asian Studies, University of Michigan, 65–80.

Magcamit, M. & A. Arugay. 2017. Rodrigo Duterte and the Making of a Populist Demigod: Part 1. *Asia Dialogue* (March 17): https://theasiadialogue.com/2017/03/17/rodrigo-duterte-and-the-making-of-a-populist-demigod-part-1/.

Marcos, F. E. 1974. *The Democratic Revolution in the Philippines*. Englewood Cliffs: Prentice-Hall International.

Maru, D. 2018. CHR Chief: Drug War Deaths Could Be as High as 27,000. *ABS-CBN News* (December 5): https://news.abs-cbn.com/focus/12/05/18/ chr-chief-drug-war-deaths-could-be-as-high-as-27000.

Maxwell, S. R. 2019. Perceived Threat of Crime, Authoritarianism, and the Rise of a Populist President in the Philippines. *International Journal of Comparative and Applied Criminal Justice* 43(3), 207–218.

May, R. J. 1992. Vigilantes in the Philippines: From Fanatical Cults to Citizens' Organizations. Philippine Studies Occasional Paper, no. 12, Center for Philippine Studies, University of Hawaii at Manoa.

Mediansky, F. A. 1986. The New People's Army: A Nation-Wide Insurgency in the Philippines. *Contemporary Southeast Asia* 8(1), 1–17.

McCoy, A. 1989. Quezon's Commonwealth. In R. R. Paredes, eds., *Philippine Colonial Democracy*. New Haven: Yale University Press, 114–160.

2001. Dark Legacy: Human Rights under the Marcos Regime. In *Memory, Truth-Telling, and the Pursuit of Justice: A Conference on the Legacies of the Marcos Dictatorship*. Quezon City: Office of Research and Publications, Ateneo de Manila University, 129–144.

2017. Global Populism: A Lineage of Filipino Strongmen from Quezon to Marcos and Duterte. *Kasarinlan* 32(1–2), 7–54.

McKenna, T. M. 1998. *Muslim Rulers and Rebels: Everyday Politics and Armed Separatism in the Southern Philippines*. Berkeley: University of California Press.

Mendoza, D. J. & M. R. Thompson. 2018. Congress: Separate but Not Equal. In M. R. Thompson & E. V. C. Batalla, eds., *Routledge Handbook of the Contemporary Philippines*. London: Routledge, 107–117.

Mendoza, R. 2018. Unmasking Duterte's Populism: Populist Rhetoric versus Policies in the Philippines. In C. Echle, F. Kliem & M. Sarmah, eds., *Panorama: Insights into Asian and European Affairs*. Singapore: Konrad Adenauer Stiftung, 67–80.

Mendoza, R. U. & D. L. Romano. 2020. The Philippines Anti-Terrorism Act: Who Guards the Guardians? *The Diplomat* (July 6): https://thediplomat.com/2020/ 07/the-philippines-anti-terrorism-act-who-guards-the-guardians/.

Mercado, M. A., ed. 1986. *People Power: The Greatest Democracy Ever Told: The Philippine Revolution of 1986 – An Eyewitness to History*. Quezon City: James B. Reuter Foundation.

Mercado, N. A. 2022. Bongbong Marcos: "The Philippines Has No Intention of Rejoining ICC." *Philippine Daily Inquirer* (August 1): https://globalnation

.inquirer.net/205693/bongbong-marcos-the-philippines-has-no-intention-of-rejoining-icc#ixzz7aicNjWjB.

Mietzner, M. 2014. Indonesia's 2014 Elections: How Jokowi Won and Democracy Survived. *Journal of Democracy* 25(4), 111–125.

Mijares, P. 1976. *The Conjugal Dictatorship of Ferdinand and Imelda Marcos.* San Francisco: Union Square.

Miller, J. 2018. *Rodrigo Duterte: Fire and Fury in the Philippines.* Melbourne: Scribe.

Mills, C. W. 1956. *The Power Elite.* New York: Oxford University Press.

Mishra, P. 2016. The Globalization of Rage. *Foreign Affairs* 95(6), 46–54.

Montiel, C. J., J. Uyheng & N. de Leon. 2021. Presidential Profanity in Duterte's Philippines: How Swearing Discursively Constructs a Populist Regime. *Journal of Language and Social Psychology* 41(4): https://doi .org/10.1177/0261927X211065780.

Mounk, Y. 2018. *The People vs. Democracy: Why Our Freedom Is in Danger and How to Save It.* Cambridge, MA: Harvard University Press.

Munro, R. H. 1985. The New Khmer Rouge. *Commentary* (December): www .commentary.org/articles/ross-munro/the-new-khmer-rouge/.

National Historical Institute. 1990. Juan Sumulong. In *Filipinos in History: Vol. II.* Manila: National Historical Institute, 225–228.

Narag, R. 2017. Failure of the Legal System: A Challenge to Filipino Lawyers. *Rappler* (August 7): www.rappler.com/thought-leaders/177893-failure-legal-system-challenge-filipino-lawyers.

Nowak, T. & K. Snyder. 1974. Clientelist Politics in the Philippines: Integration or Instability? *The American Political Science Review* 68(3), 1147–1170.

Ong, J. C. & J. V. A. Cabañes. 2018. Architects of Networked Disinformation: Behind the Scenes of Troll Accounts and Fake News. University of Massachusetts Amherst, Communication Department Faculty Publication: https://scholarworks.umass.edu/cgi/viewcontent.cgi?article=1075& context=communication_faculty_pubs.

Ong, J. C. & J. V. A. Cabañes. 2019. When Disinformation Studies Meets Production Studies: Social Identities and Moral Justifications in the Political Trolling Industry. *International Journal of Communication* 13 (1), 5771–5790.

Ong, J. C., R. Tapsell & N. Curato. 2019. Tracking Digital Disinformation in the 2019 Philippine Midterm Election. *New Mandala* (August): www.new mandala.org/wp-content/uploads/2019/08/Digital-Disinformation-2019-Midterms.pdf.

Ordoñez, M. & A. Borja. 2018. Philippine Liberal Democracy under Siege: The Ideological Underpinnings of Duterte's Populist Challenge. *Philippine Political Science Journal* 39(2), 139–153.

Paredes, R. R. 1989. The Paradox of Colonial Democracy. In R. R. Paredes, ed., *Philippine Colonial Democracy*. Quezon City: Ateneo de Manila University Press, 1–19.

Parmanand, S. 2020. The Dangers of Masculinity Contests in a Time of Pandemic. *Oxford Political Review* (April 18): https://oxfordpoliticalreview.com/2020/04/18/the-dangers-of-masculinity-contests-in-a-time-of-pandemic/.

Parreño, E. G. 2019. *Beyond Will and Power: A Biography of President Rodrigo Roa Duterte*. Lapulapu City: Optima.

Pavin, C. 2019. Why Thailand's New Military-Monarchy Alliance Is a Bad Sign for Democracy. *The Diplomat* (June 21): https://thediplomat.com/2019/06/why-thailands-new-military-monarchy-alliance-is-a-bad-sign-for-democracy/.

PCIJ Staff. 2022. Marcos Promises Financial Aid and Land Distribution to Revive Agri Sector. *Philippine Center for Investigative Journalism* (July 25): https://pcij.org/article/8998/live-blog-marcos-sona-state-of-the-nation-address.

Peel, M. 2017. Drugs and Death in Davao: The Making of Rodrigo Duterte. *Financial Times* (February 2): www.ft.com/content/9d6225dc-e805-11e6-967b-c88452263daf.

Pepinsky, T. 2017. Southeast Asia: Voting against Disorder. *Journal of Democracy* 28(2), 120–131.

Pernia, A. 2021. Authoritarian Values and Institutional Trust: Theoretical Considerations and Evidence from the Philippines. *Asian Journal of Comparative Politics* 7(2), 204–232.

Philippine Center for Investigative Journalism. 2017. What's Flawed, Fuzzy with Drug War Numbers? *Philippine Center for Investigative Journalism* (June 8): https://pcij.org/stories/pcij-findings-whats-flawed-fuzzy-with-drug.

Philippine Statistics Authority. 2002. 2000 Family Income and Expenditures Survey (FIES) Final Release on Poverty (April 16): https://psa.gov.ph/content/2000-family-income-and-expenditures-survey-fies-final-release-poverty#:~:text=POVERTY%20INCIDENCE,to%2039.4%20percent%20in%202000.

Prajak K. 2014. The Rise and Fall of Electoral Violence in Thailand: Changing Rules, Structures and Power Landscapes, 1997–2011. *Contemporary Southeast Asia* 36(3), 386–416

Pratt, J. 2007. *Penal Populism*. London: Routledge.

Punongbayan, J. 2019a. How the TRAIN Law Worsened Poverty, Inequality. *Rappler* (April 25): www.rappler.com/thought-leaders/228952-how-tax-reform-law-worsened-poverty-inequality-philippines.

2019b. Why the Free Tuition Law Is Not Pro-Poor Enough. *Rappler* (February 8): www.rappler.com/thought-leaders/222981-analysis-reasons-free-tuition-law-not-pro-poor-enough.

2020. How Data Debunk Duterte's Toxic "Pasaway" Narrative. *Rappler* (June 22): www.rappler.com/voices/thought-leaders/analysis-how-datade bunk-duterte-toxic-pasaway-narrative.

Putzel, J. A. 1992. *A Captive Land: The Politics of Agrarian Reform in the Philippines*. New York: Monthly Press.

2020. The "Populist" Right Challenge to Neoliberalism: Social Policy between a Rock and a Hard Place. *Development and Change* 51, 418–441.

Quimpo, N. G. 2008. *Contested Democracy and the Left in the Philippines after Marcos*. Quezon City: Ateneo d Manila University Press.

2017. Duterte's "War on Drugs": The Securitization of Illegal Drugs and the Return of National Boss Rule. In N. Curato, ed., *A Duterte Reader: Critical Essays on Rodrigo Duterte's Early Presidency*. Quezon City: Ateneo de Manila Press, 145–166.

2021. The Limits of Duterte's Power. *Rappler* (March 26): www.rappler .com/voices/thought-leaders/opinion-limits-duterte-power/.

Raffle, E. 2021. The War on Drugs in Southeast Asia as "State Vigilantism." *International Journal of Drug Policy*: https://doi.org/10.1016/j.drugpo .2021.103114.

Ramos, C. G. 2021. The Return of Strongman Rule in the Philippines: Neoliberal Roots and Developmental Implications. *Geoforum* (April 18): www.sciencedirect.com/science/article/abs/pii/S0016718521001007.

Ranada, P. 2021a. Some Pro-Duterte Personalities Bash Aquino Even in Death. *Rappler* (June 24): www.rappler.com/nation/duterte-supporters-bash-noy noy-aquino-even-death/.

2021b. Duterte May Cap Term as Most Popular Philippine President. *Rappler* (June 30): www.rappler.com/newsbreak/in-depth/so-what-if-duterte-may-cap-term-as-philippines-most-popular-president/.

Rappler Investigative Team. 2021a. The Lascañas Affidavit – "I killed for Duterte." *Rappler* (November 10): www.rappler.com/newsbreak/investigative/ arthur-lascanas-icc-affidavit-series-i-killed-for-duterte/.

2021b. Duterte as "Superman": Lascañas Details Davao Death Squad Operations. *Rappler* (November 16): www.rappler.com/newsbreak/iq/ duterte-superman-arthur-lascanas-details-davao-death-squad-operations.

Raquiza, A. R. 1997. The Social Reform Agenda. *Social Watch*: www.social watch.org/node /10602.

2018. The Changing Configuration of Philippine Capitalism. In M. R. Thompson & E. V. C. Batalla, eds., *Routledge Handbook of the Contemporary Philippines*. London: Routledge, 235–254.

Raquiza, M. 2018. The Allure of Pantawid Pamilya: The Conditional Cash Transfer Scheme. In M. R. Thompson & E. V. C. Batalla, eds., *Routledge Handbook of the Contemporary Philippines*. London: Routledge, 273–283.

2019. SDG 8 and 10: Growth, Labor Productivity and Decent Work: What Needs to Happen to Reduce Poverty and Inequality in the Philippines. In *Social Watch Philippines, The PH SDG Agenda: Closing Gaps, Overcoming Policy Incoherence*. Quezon City: Social Watch Philippines, University of the Philippines, 10–45.

Regalado, E. 2021. Noy, Rody Ties Date Back to Davao "Yellow Fridays." *The Philippine Star* (June 28): www.pressreader.com/philippines/the-philippine-star/20210628/281509344159361.

Regilme, S. S. F. 2021a. Visions of Peace amidst a Human Rights Crisis: War on Drugs in Colombia and the Philippines. *Journal of Global Security Studies* 6(2) https: ogaa022, https://doi.org/10.1093/jogss/ogaa022.

2021b. Contested Spaces of Illiberal and Authoritarian Politics: Human Rights and Democracy in Crisis. *Political Geography* 89: https://doi.org/10.1016/j.polgeo.2021.102427.

Republic of the Philippines Supreme Court. 2018. G.R. No. 234359 (AILEEN ALMORA, ET AL. v. DIRECTOR GENERAL RONALD DELA ROSA, in his capacity as Chief of the Philippine National Police, ET AL.), en banc resolution (April 3): https://lawphil.net/sc_res/2018/pdf/gr_234359_2018.pdf.

Reyes, D. 2016. The Spectacle of Violence in Duterte's "War on Drugs". *Journal of Current Southeast Asian Affairs* 35(3), 111–137.

2022. The Persistence of Political Violence in the Philippines after the Fall of the Marcos Dictatorship. PhD dissertation, City University of Hong Kong.

Reyes, M. P. P. 2019. The Duterte-Marcos Connection. *ABS-CBN News* (September 30): https://news.abs-cbn.com/spotlight/09/30/19/the-duterte-marcos-connection.

Riedinger, J. M. 1995. *Agrarian Reform in the Philippines: Democratic Transitions and Redistributive Reform*. Stanford: Stanford University Press.

Rimban, L. 2011. Breaking the Cycle of Electoral Violence. In Y. Chua & L. Rimban, eds., *Democracy at Gunpoint: Election-Related Violence in the Philippines*. Makati: The Asia Foundation, i–xxi.

Robles, A. 2019. The Philippines' Communist Rebellion Is Asia's Longest-Running Insurgency. *South China Morning Post* (September 16): www.scmp.com/week-asia/politics/article/3027414/explained-philippines-communist-rebellion-asias-longest-running.

Rodan, G. 2021. Inequality and Political Representation in the Philippines and Singapore. *Journal of Contemporary Asia* 51(2), 233–261.

Ronas, M. C. 2016. The Never Ending Democratization of the Philippines. In F. B. Miranda & T. C. Rivera, eds., *Chasing the Wind: Assessing Philippine Democracy*, 2nd ed. Quezon City: Commission on Human Rights and the United Nations Development Programme, 75–106.

Rose-Ackerman, S. & D. A. Desierto. 2011. Hyper-presidentialism: Separation of Powers without Checks and Balances in Argentina and Philippines. *Berkeley Journal of International Law* 29, 246–333.

Rosenberg, D. 1979. Liberty versus Loyalty. In D. Rosenberg, ed., *Marcos and Martial Law in the Philippines*. Ithaca: Cornell University Press, 145–179.

Rufo, A. C. 2013. *Altar of Secrets: Sex, Politics, and Money in the Philippine Catholic Church*. Manila: Journalism for Nation Building Foundation.

Sanchez, M. 2017. Human Rights and the Task Force Detainees of the Philippines: Religious Opposition to the Marcos Dictatorship, 1972–1986. *Kritika Kultura* 29, 126–156.

Sarao, Z. G. H. 2021. PH Ranks Last Out of 121 Countries in Global COVID-19 Recovery Index – Nikkei. *Philippine Daily Inquirer* (October 6): www .newsinfo.inquirer.net/1498167/ph-ranks-last-out-of-121-countries-in-global-covid-19-recovery-index-nikkei.

Scalice, J. P. 2017. Crisis of Revolutionary Leadership: Martial Law and the Communist Parties of the Philippines, 1959–1974. PhD dissertation, University of California.

    2020. First as Tragedy, Second as Farce: Marcos, Duterte and the Communist Parties of the Philippines. Lecture at the Nanyang Technological University, Singapore (August 26): https://libcom.org/article/first-tragedy-second-farce-marcos-duterte-and-communist-parties-philippines.

Shain, Y. & M. R. Thompson. 1990. The Role of Political Exiles in Democratic Transition: The Case of the Philippines. *Journal of Developing Societies* VI, 71–86.

Sidel, J. T. 1999. *Capital, Coercion, and Crime: Bossism in the Philippines*. Stanford: Stanford University Press.

    2012. Economic Foundations of Subnational Authoritarianism: Insights and Evidence from Qualitative and Quantitative Research. *Democratization* 21 (1), 161–184.

    2016. The Philippines' New President: One Step Backward, Two Steps Forward? *Europe's World* (June 6): https://europesworld.org/2016/06/06/philippines-new-president-one-stepbackward-two-steps-forward/# .V9Ff9TW3vVI.

Simangan, D. 2018. Is the Philippine "War on Drugs" an Act of Genocide? *Journal of Genocide Research* 20(1), 68–89.

Slayton G. & M. R. Thompson. 1985. An Essay on Credit Arrangements between the IMF and the Republic of the Philippines: 1970–1983. *Philippine Review of Economics and Business* XXII(1–2), 59–81.

Social Weather Stations. 2021. Third Quarter 2021 Social Weather Survey: 45% of Filipino Familes Feel Poor, 34% Feel Borderline Poor, 21% Feel not Poor (November 27): www.sws.org.ph/swsmain/artcldisppage/?artcsyscode=ART-20211127144913.

Starner, F. L. 1961. *Magsaysay and the Philippines Peasantry: The Agrarian Impact on Philippine Politics, 1953–1956.* Berkeley: University of California Press.

Stauffer, R. B. 1981. The Politics of Becoming: The Mindanao Conflict in a World-System Perspective. *Dependency Series: Third World Studies Center*, no. 31. Quezon City: University of the Philippines.

Sturtevant, D. 1976. *Popular Uprisings in the Philippines: 1840–1940.* Ithaca: Cornell University Press.

Suorsa, O. & M. Thompson. 2018. Choosing Sides? Illiberal Realignment and Hedging in the Philippines and Thailand. In *Panorama – Insights into Asia and European Affairs.* Singapore: Konrad Adenauer Stiftung, 63–76: www.kas.de/c/document_library/get_file?uuid=22f22081-a5f9-5472-6368-24716055e41f&groupId=288143.

Szilágyi. A. & M. R. Thompson. 2016. Digong and the Donald: The Indiscreet Charm of Informality in Politics. *Rappler* (November 16): www.rappler.com/voices/thought-leaders/154066-digong-donald-trump-informality-language/.

Takagi, Y. 2017. Policy Coalitions and Ambitious Politicians: A Case Study of Philippine Social Policy Reform. *Philippine Political Science Journal* 38 (1), 28–47.

Takigawa, T. 1964. Landownership and Land Reform Problems of the Philippines. *The Developing Economies* 2, 58–77.

Talabong, R. 2020. Over 100,000 Quarantine Violators Arrested in PH since March. *Rappler* (September 8): www.rappler.com/nation/arrested-quarantine-violators-philippines-2020.

Talamayan, F. 2019. Nostalgia, Conspiracies: The Politics of Recalling the Marcos "Golden Age." *Rappler* (December 15): www.rappler.com/voices/imho/opinion-nostalgia-conspiracies-politics-remembering-marcos-golden-age.

    2021. The Politics of Nostalgia and the Marcos Golden Age in the Philippines. *Asia Review* 11(3), 273–304: https://snuac.snu.ac.kr/2015.

Teehankee, J. C. 2016. Weak State, Strong Presidents: Situating the Duterte Presidency in Philippine Political Time. *Journal of Developing Societies* 32, 293–321.

2019. Duterte's Federalist Project Indefinitely on Hold. *East Asia Forum* (July 24): www.eastasiaforum.org/2019/07/24/dutertes-federalist-project-indefinitely-on-hold/.

2020. Duterte's COVID-19 Powers and the Paradox of the Philippine Presidency. *CSEAS-Kyoto* (April 28): https://covid-19chronicles.cseas.kyoto-u.ac.jp/post-007.html?fbclid=IwAR2-swiSiI-ehgjzSThLj5Tng0mmwhv35T0qi6 HeoEt_4zDRRXKH2cYLZ8.

Teehankee, J. C. & C. A. A. Calimbahin. 2022. *Patronage Democracy in the Philippines: Clans, Clients, and Competition in Local Elections.* Quezon City: Ateneo de Manila Press.

Teehankee, J. C. & M. R. Thompson. 2016. The Vote in the Philippines: Electing a Strongman. *Journal of Democracy* 27(4), 124–134.

Terami-Wada, M. 1988. The Sakdal Movement, 1930–34. *Philippine Studies* 36 (2), 131–150.

Thompson, M. R. 1995. *The Anti-Marcos Struggle: Personalistic Rule and Democratic Transition in the Philippines.* New Haven: Yale University Press and Juan J. Linz

1998. The Marcos Regime in the Philippines. In H. E. Chehabi, ed., *Sultanistic Regimes.* Baltimore: Johns Hopkins University Press, 206–229.

2004. *Democratic Revolutions: Asia and Eastern Europe.* London: Routledge.

2007. *Presidentas* and People Power in Comparative Asian Perspective. *Philippine Political Science Journal* 28(51), 1–32.

2008. People Power Sours: Uncivil Society in Thailand and the Philippines. *Current History* 107 (712), 381–387.

2010. Populism and the Revival of Reform: Competing Narratives in the Philippines. *Contemporary Southeast Asia* 32(1), 1–28.

2014a. The Politics Philippine Presidents Make: Presidential Style, Patronage-Based or Regime Relational? *Critical Asian Studies* 46, 433–460.

2014b. Aquino's Reformism Hits a Dead End. *East Asia Forum* (September 30): www.eastasiaforum.org/2014/09/30/aquinos-reformism-hits-a-dead-end/.

2016. Poor Filipinos' Lives Don't Seem to Matter. *New Mandala* (August 12): www.newmandala.org/poor-filipinos-lives-dont-seem-matter/.

2018. Why Duterte Remains So Popular: The Failures of the Philippine's Liberal Reformism. *Foreign Affairs* (October 9): www.foreignaffairs.com/articles/philippines/2018-10-09/why-duterte-remains-so-popular.

2019. The Rise of Illiberal Democracy in the Philippines: Duterte's Early Presidency. In I. Deinla & B. Dressel, eds., *From Aquino II to Duterte (2010–18): Change, Continuity – and Rupture*. Singapore: ISEAS, 39–61.

2021. Pushback after Backsliding? Unconstrained Executive Aggrandizement in the Philippines versus Contested Military-Monarchical Rule in Thailand. *Democratization* 28(1), 124–141.

2022a. Duterte's Violent Populism: Mass Murder, Political Legitimacy and the "Death of Development" in the Philippines. *Journal of Contemporary Asia* 52(3), 403–428.

2022b. Brute Force Governance: Public Approval despite Policy Failure during the COVID-19 Pandemic in the Philippines. *Journal of Current Southeast Asian Affairs* 41(3), 399–421: https://doi.org/10.1177/186810 34221092453.

2022c. Whatever Happened to the "Aircon Opposition" to Marcos? Or, How the "Yellows" Turned Pink with Embarrassment. In L. Castañeda Anastacio & P. N. Abinales, eds., *The Marcos Era: A Reader*. Quezon City: Ateneo de Manila University Press, 178–200.

Tiglao, R. 2013. DBM Data Confirm P100M "Bribe" to 16 Senators Each. *Rigobertotiglao* (October 3): www.rigobertotiglao.com/2013/10/03/dbm-data-confirm-p100m-bribe-to-16-senators-each/.

2016. Only Binay and Roxas have Electoral Machinery. *Manila Times* (April 3): www.manilatimes.net/only-binay-and-roxas-have-electoral-machinery/253878/.

2022a. Marcos' Landslide Victory Inevitable. *Manila Times* (May 11): www.manilatimes.net/2022/05/11/opinion/columns/marcos-landslide-victory-inevitable/1843198.

2022b. The End of the Yellows and Pinks, and What It Means. *Manila Times* (May 20): www.manilatimes.net/2022/05/20/opinion/columns/the-end-of-the-yellows-and-pinks-and-what-it-means/1844340.

Tigno, J. V. 2018. Ricardo R. Pascual (1912–1985): Partyless Democracy. In J. V. Tigno, ed., *Twentieth Century Political Thinkers in the Philippines*. Quezon City: University of the Philippines Press, 104–112.

Timberman, D. G. 1991. *A Changeless Land: Continuity and Change in the Philippines*. Singapore: Institute of Southeast Asian Studies.

2019. Philippine Politics Under Duterte: A Midterm Assessment. *Carnegie Endowment for Peace* (January 10): https://carnegieendowment.org/2019/01/10/philippine-politics-under-duterte-midterm-assessment-pub-78091.

Tuminez, A. S. 2007. This Land Is Our Land: Moro Ancestral Domain and Its Implications for Peace and Development in the Southern Philippines. *The SAIS Review of International Affairs* 27(2), 77–91.

Tupaz, V. 2015. State of Hacienda Luisita. *Rappler* (July 27): www.rappler
.com/moveph/100628-state-hacienda-luisita/.

Tuquero, L. 2022. Duterte "Institutionalized" Disinformation, Paved the Way for
a Marcos Victory. *Rappler* (June 19): www.rappler.com/newsbreak/in-depth/
duterte-institutionalized-disinformation-paved-way-marcos-jr-victory-2022/.

United Nations High Commissioner on Human Rights. 2020. Situation of
Human Rights in the Philippines. *Report of the United Nations High
Commissioner for Human Rights* (June 29): www.ohchr.org/sites/default/
files/Documents/Countries/PH/Philippines-HRC44-AEV.pdf.

van der Kamp, D. 2021. Blunt Force Regulation and Bureaucratic Control:
Understanding China's War on Pollution. *Governance* 34(1), 191–209.

van der Kroef, J. M. 1988. The Philippines: Day of the Vigilantes. *Asian Survey*
28(6), 630–649.

van Krieken, R. 2017. Norbert Elias and Figurational Sociology. In
B. S. Turner, ed., *The Wiley-Blackwell Encyclopedia of Social Theory*.
Hoboken: Wiley-Blackwell.

Vartavarian, M. 2019a. Parsing People's War: Militias and Counterinsurgencies
in the Philippines. *Kyoto Review* (July): https://kyotoreview.org/trendsetters/
militias-and-counterinsurgencies-in-the-philippines/.

2019b. A Tale of Two Warlords: Andal Ampatuan, Rodrigo Duterte, and the
Philippines' Mutating Politics. *Forsea* (November 29): https://forsea.co/
philippines-tale-of-two-warlords/.

Vera Files. 2022. Vera Files Fact Sheet: Disparity in Body Count of Drug War
Victims Explained (December 13): https://verafiles.org/articles/vera-files-
fact-sheet-disparity-in-body-count-of-drug-war-victims-explained.

Vitug, M. 2016. The Scrum: Roxas, Binay and the Political Machine. *Rappler*
(April 20): www.rappler.com/nation/politics/elections/2016/129982-
roxas-binay-political-machine.

Warburg, A. & S. Jensen. 2018. Policing the War on Drugs and the
Transformation of Urban Space in Manila. *Environment and Planning
D: Society and Space* 38(3), 399–416.

Webb A. 2017. Why Are the Middle Class Misbehaving? Exploring Democratic
Ambivalence and Authoritarian Nostalgia. *Philippine Sociological Review*
65, 77–102.

Weekley, K. 2001. *The Communist Party of the Philippines 1968–1993: A Story
of Its Theory and Practice*. Quezon City: University of the Philippine Press.

Williams, S. 2018. How the Catholic Church Is Fighting the Drug War in the
Philippines. *American Magazine* (January 25): www.americamagazine
.org/politics-society/2018/01/25/how-catholic-church-fighting-drug-war-
philippines.

Williamson, J. G. & E. S. de Dios. 2014. Has the Philippines Forever Lost Its Chance at Industrialization? *The Philippine Review of Economics* LI(2), 47–66.

Winters, J. 2011. *Oligarchy.* Cambridge: Cambridge University Press.

Wodak, R. 2015. *The Politics of Fear.* London: Sage.

Wong, E. 2022. In the Philippines, Blinken Vows to Strengthen Military Ties. *New York Times* (August 6): www.nytimes.com/2022/08/06/world/asia/blinken-philippines-us-asia-tensions.html?searchResultPosition=1.

Wurfel, D. 1958. Philippine Agrarian Reform under Magsaysay. *Far Eastern Survey* 27(1): https://davidwurfel.ca/philippine-agrarian-reform-under-magsaysay.

　1988. *Filipino Politics: Development and Decay.* Ithaca: Cornell University Press.

Yap, C. & A. Calonzo. 2022. News Site Run by Nobel Prize Winner Faces Closure in Philippines. *Bloomberg* (June 29): www.bloomberg.com/news/articles/2022-06-29/philippine-news-site-rappler-faces-closure-as-sec-order-affirmed#xj4y7vzkg.

Acknowledgments

I wish to thank the series editors, Ed Aspinall and Meredith Weiss, for entrusting me with this Element project which had to be completed under a tight schedule. Three anonymous reviewers provided valuable criticisms and suggestions. The work draws on the long years of research on Philippine politics for which I have accumulated many debts of gratitude. I wish to make special mention of my late friend Jose Luis Martin C. "Chito" Gascon whose courage continues to inspire me. Many thanks are due longtime friends in the Philippines and/or Philippine studies friends (among them former classmates and mentors) as well as more recent acquaintances from whom I have learned much: Patricio N. Abinales, Carmel V. Abao, Aries Arugay, Maria Ela L. Atienza, Alfredo I. Ayala, Manuel I. Ayala, Coeli Barry, Eric Vicente C. Batalla, Walden Bello, Anthony Lawrence A. Borja, Vincent G. Boudreau, Cleo Anne A. Calimbahin, Renato Cruz de Castro, Lisandro E. Claudio, Kit Collier, Antonio P. Contreras, Nicole Curato, Randolf S. David, Karen S. Gomez Dumpit, Jean S. Encinas-Franco, Manfred Fuchs, Ramon Guillermo, Rosalie Arcala Hall, Caroline Hau, Eva-Lotta E. Hedman, Carolina G. Hernandez, Alan Hicken, Ronald D. Holmes, Paul D. Hutchcroft, Sol Iglesias, Bonn Juego, Yuko Kasuya, Benedict J. Kerkvliet, Masataka Kimura, Gilbert Legaspi, Howard Loewen, Francisco A. Magno, Michael J. Montesano, Fidel R. Nemenzo, Francisco Nemenzo, Jr., Jonathan C. Ong, Matthew Ordonez, Sharmila Parmanand, Nathan G. Quimpo, Antoinette R. Raquiza, Mina Roces, Garry Rodan, Ranjit S. Rye, Horacio G. Severino, John T. Sidel, Gregory Slayton, Allen B. Surla, Anna Szilágyi, Eduardo C. Tadem, Teresa S. Encarnacion Tadem, Yusuke Takagi, Rolando G. Talampas, Julio C. Teehankee, Rosa Babel C. Teehankee, Jorge V. Tigno, David G. Timberman, Ador R. Torneo, and Franco Villanueva. I would also like to thank the PhD students I have supervised, from whom I have gained much insight into Philippine politics and society – Kevin Nielsen M. Agojo, Roger Chao, Lermie Shayne S. Garcia, Ina Karas, Diana J. Mendoza, Marivic Victoria R. Raquiza, and Danilo A. Reyes. I also wish to acknowledge research support from the Hong Kong Research Grants Council, General Research Fund (#11600921).

Cambridge Elements ≡

Politics and Society in Southeast Asia

Edward Aspinall

Australian National University

Edward Aspinall is a professor of politics at the Coral Bell School of Asia-Pacific Affairs, Australian National University. A specialist of Southeast Asia, especially Indonesia, much of his research has focused on democratisation, ethnic politics and civil society in Indonesia and, most recently, clientelism across Southeast Asia.

Meredith L. Weiss

University at Albany, SUNY

Meredith L. Weiss is Professor of Political Science at the University at Albany, SUNY. Her research addresses political mobilization and contention, the politics of identity and development, and electoral politics in Southeast Asia, with particular focus on Malaysia and Singapore.

About the Series

The Elements series Politics and Society in Southeast Asia includes both country-specific and thematic studies on one of the world's most dynamic regions. Each title, written by a leading scholar of that country or theme, combines a succinct, comprehensive, up-to-date overview of debates in the scholarly literature with original analysis and a clear argument.

Cambridge Elements ≡

Politics and Society in Southeast Asia

Printed in the United States
by Baker & Taylor Publisher Services